GOOD DRINKS

GOOD DRINKS

Ambrose Heath

LONDON
FABER & FABER LTD.

First published in 1939
by Faber & Faber Limited
Bloomsbury House
74–77 Great Russell Street
London WC1B 3DA
This edition first published in 2015

Printed and bound by CPI Group (UK) Ltd, Croydon CR0 4YY

A CIP record for this book
is available from the British Library

ISBN 978–0–571–32393–7

FSC
www.fsc.org
MIX
Paper from
responsible sources
FSC® C101712

2 4 6 8 10 9 7 5 3 1

To All Good
BOON-COMPANIONS

FOREWORD

This collection of divers drinks is offered for all those occasions when drinking is desirable: on a winter's evening by the fire, on the shady verge of the tennis-court, at a party, in a pub; with friends, or acquaintances and those even dearer, wherever they may happen to be together: to the advancement of the brewer and the wine merchant, and the confusion of all dull dogs.

A.H.

Holmbury St. Mary
June 1939

CONTENTS

FOREWORD *page* 7

A SMALL COLLECTION OF QUOTATIONS APPOSITE
    TO THE CONTENTS OF THIS BOOK   11

Part I. HARD DRINKS

1. COCKTAILS	21
2. COLD DRINKS	43
3. HOT DRINKS	69
4. CUPS	83
5. PUNCHES	99
6. LIQUEURS	111
7. HOME-MADE DRINKS	115
8. VEGETABLE WINES	139
9. CURIOUS DRINKS	147
10. A NOTE ON WINE	155

Part II. SOFT DRINKS

11. COCKTAILS	161
12. COLD DRINKS	169
13. HOT DRINKS	183

CONTENTS

14. CUPS	*page* 189	
15. PUNCHES	195	
16. COLD MILK DRINKS	203	
17. HOT MILK DRINKS	209	
18. FRUIT MILK DRINKS	215	
19. INVALID DRINKS	219	
APPENDIX	226	
INDEX	231	

A SMALL COLLECTION OF
QUOTATIONS APPOSITE TO
THE CONTENTS OF THIS BOOK

It has become popular of late to enter into friendly competition over quotations, pieces of music, fragments of general knowledge, noises, and so on. The following quotations are not intended to tax the knowledge of users of this book, but are meant to afford amusement or pleasure. Those, however, who possess the acquisitive type of mind may care to turn to page 230, where they will find a list of the authors.

1.   A bumper of good liquor
            Will end a contest quicker
            Than Justice, Judge or Vicar.

2. Oh, some that's good and godly ones they holds
        that it's a sin
    To troll the jolly bowl around, and let the
        dollars spin;
    But I'm for toleration and for drinking at an
        inn. . . .

3.   The rapturous, wild and ineffable pleasure
      Of drinking at somebody else's expense.

4.   Glass of Brandy and Water! That is the current but not the appropriate name; ask for a glass of liquid fire and distilled damnation!

5.   If I had a thousand sons, the first human principle I would teach them should be—to forswear thin potations.

6.   If on my theme I rightly think,
      There are five reasons why men drink——
      Good wine, a friend, because I'm dry,
      Or lest I should be by and by,
      Or any other reason why.

7. Si bene commemini, causae sunt quinque
       bibendi.
   Hospitis adventus; praesens sitis atque futura;
   Et vini bonitas, aut quaelibet altera causae.

8.   A man cannot make him laugh—but that's no marvel; he drinks no wine.

9.   To drink is a Christian diversion,
      Unknown to the Turk or the Persian.

10.   Man wants but little drink below,
    But wants that little strong.

11.   There are two reasons for drinking; one is, when you are thirsty, to cure it; the other, when you are not thirsty, to prevent it. . . . Prevention is better than cure.

12.   'I rather like bad wine,' said Mr. Mount-chesney; 'one gets so bored with good wine.'

13.   'It wasn't the wine,' said Mr. S—— in a broken voice. 'It was the salmon.'

14.   And took more Port than was exactly portable.

15.   From the town all Inns have been driven: from the villages most. . . . Change your hearts or you will lose your Inns and you will deserve to have lost them. But when you have lost your Inns, drown your empty selves, for you will have lost the last of England.

16.   Life is with such all beer and skittles;
    They are not difficult to please
    About their victuals.

17. Here sleeps in peace a Hampshire grenadier,
Who caught his death by drinking cold small
    beer.
Soldier, take heed from his untimely fall,
And when you're hot, drink strong or not
    at all.

18. Three cups of this a prudent man may take;
The first of these for constitution's sake,
The second to the lass he loves the best,
The third and last to lull him to his rest.

19. But punch, my dear C——, like time and
tide, waits for no man.

20. Claret is the liquor for boys; port for men;
but he who aspires to be a hero must drink brandy.

21. To ask you to dinner without a drink is to
ask you to half a dinner.

22. Drinks for one day at Brighton (having
nothing to do):

> Hollands Gin
> Rum and Milk   } before Breakfast
> Coffee (Breakfast)
> Hollands
> Porter   } before Dinner

Shrub
Ale
Hollands and Water   } before Dinner
Port Wine with Ginger
Bottled Porter
Port Wine (at Dinner and after)
Porter
Bottled Porter
Punch
Porter
Ale
Opium and Water
Port Wine (at Supper)
Gin and Water
Shrub
Rum on going to Bed.

23. A neat glass of *parfait d'amour*, which one sips
    Just as if boiled velvet tripped over one's lips.

24. When you and I went down the lane with ale
        mugs in our hands,
    The night we went to Glastonbury by way of
        Goodwin Sands.

25.   Without any doubt whatsoever this nectar
was brewed in the waxing of the moon and of that
barley which Brutus brought hither in the first

founding of this land! And the water wherein that barley-corn was brewed was May-day dew, the dew upon the grass before the sunrise of a May-day morning. For it has all the seven qualities of ale, which are:

Aleph	..	Clarity.
Beth	..	Savour.
Gimel	..	A lively hue.
Daleth	..	Lightness.
He	..	Profundity.
Vau	..	Strength retained.

and lastly, Zayin, which is Perfection and The End. . . . It is indeed good beer; and when we leave our valleys we will all drink it together in Paradise.

PART I
HARD DRINKS

COCKTAILS

COCKTAILS

ABSINTHE

½ Absinthe
½ Water
1 dash Syrup
1 dash Angostura Bitters

ALEXANDRA

⅓ Gin
⅓ Curaçao
⅓ Cream

AMERICAN BEAUTY

1 dash Crème de Menthe
¼ Orange juice
¼ Grenadine
¼ French Vermouth
¼ Brandy
When shaken and poured out, top with a little port.

COCKTAILS

ANGEL FACE

⅓ Dry Gin
⅓ Apricot Brandy
⅓ Calvados

APPLE JACK (I)

½ Calvados or Apple Jack
½ Italian Vermouth
1 Dash Angostura Bitters

APPLE JACK (II)

⅔ Apple Jack or Calvados
⅙ Grenadine
⅙ Lemon juice

APRICOT

½ Apricot Brandy
¼ Orange juice
¼ Lemon juice
1 dash Dry Gin

BARON

⅔ Dry Gin
⅓ French Vermouth
6 dashes Curaçao
2 dashes Italian Vermouth

22

COCKTAILS

BELMONT

2 Dry Gin
$\frac{1}{3}$ Grenadine
1 teaspoonful Cream

BENTLEY

$\frac{1}{2}$ Calvados or Apple Jack
$\frac{1}{2}$ Dubonnet

BITTER SWEET

$\frac{1}{3}$ Gin
$\frac{1}{6}$ Orange juice
$\frac{1}{6}$ Italian Vermouth
$\frac{1}{6}$ Bénédictine
$\frac{1}{6}$ Cherry Brandy

BLOODHOUND

$\frac{1}{2}$ Dry Gin
$\frac{1}{4}$ French Vermouth
$\frac{1}{4}$ Italian Vermouth
2 or 3 crushed Strawberries
Strain after shaking.

COCKTAILS

BLUE DEVIL

½ Dry Gin
¼ Lemon or Lime juice
¼ Maraschino
Dash blue vegetable colouring

BOBBY BURNS

½ Scotch Whisky
½ Italian Vermouth
3 dashes Bénédictine

BOMBAY

½ Brandy
¼ French Vermouth
¼ Italian Vermouth
2 dashes Curaçao
1 dash Absinthe

BOSOM CARESSER

⅔ Brandy
⅓ Curaçao
The yolk of an Egg
1 teaspoonful Grenadine

COCKTAILS

BRANDY

¾ wineglass of Brandy
2 dashes Curaçao

BRANDY COCKTAIL

2 tablespoonfuls Brandy
1 dash Orange Bitters
2 dashes Angostura Bitters
3 dashes Maraschino
A good piece of ice

BRANDY VERMOUTH

¾ Brandy
¼ Italian Vermouth
1 dash Angostura Bitters

BRAVE NEW WORLD

⅓ Passion Fruit juice
⅔ Gin
3 dashes Orange Bitters
2 dashes Angostura Bitters
  Should be well iced and shaken.

COCKTAILS

BRONX

½ Dry Gin
¼ French Vermouth
¼ Italian Vermouth
Juice of quarter of an Orange

BRONX, SILVER

As above with the addition of a white of an egg.

CALVADOS

⅓ Calvados
⅓ Orange juice
⅙ Cointreau
⅙ Orange Bitters

CHAMPAGNE COCKTAIL

Put a lump of Sugar into a wineglass and soak it
with Angostura Bitters. Add a piece of ice, fill up
with Champagne, squeeze a bit of lemon peel on
top and garnish with a slice of orange.

CINZANO

1 glass Cinzano Vermouth
2 dashes Angostura Bitters
2 dashes Orange Bitters
  Squeeze orange peel on top.

COCKTAILS

CLOVER CLUB

⅔ Dry Gin
⅓ Grenadine
The juice of half a Lemon or one Lime
1 Egg-white

CORPSE REVIVER

½ Brandy
¼ Calvados or Apple Jack
¼ Italian Vermouth

CRÉOLE

⅓ Absinthe
⅔ Italian Vermouth

DAIQUIRI

1 glass Bacardi Rum
1 teaspoonful powdered Sugar
The juice of quarter of a Lemon or half a Lime

DEVIL'S KISS

⅓ Gin
⅓ Brandy
⅙ Lemon juice
⅙ Bénédictine

27

COCKTAILS

⅙ Cointreau
2 dashes Absinthe
1 teaspoonful Grenadine

DUBONNET

½ Dubonnet
½ Dry Gin

GIN COCKTAIL

1 glass Dry Gin
4 dashes Orange Bitters

GIN AND CAPE

½ Gin
½ Caperitif
Squeeze lemon peel on top.

GIN-AND-IT

Gin with Italian Vermouth in varying proportions.

GIN AND MIXED

⅓ Gin
⅓ French Vermouth
⅓ Italian Vermouth

28

COCKTAILS

⅔ Dry Gin
⅓ French Vermouth
2 dashes Angostura Bitters

GRAPEFRUIT

3½ glasses of Gin
The juice of 1½ good-sized Grapefruit
Sugar to taste, and plenty of ice

GREEN ROOM

⅓ Brandy
⅔ French Vermouth
2 dashes Curaçao

HOLLYWOOD

⅔ Gin
⅓ fresh Cream
⅓ Grenadine

HOMESTEAD

⅔ Dry Gin
⅓ Italian Vermouth
1 slice Orange

COCKTAILS

HONEY ORANGE COCKTAIL

1½ gills Orange juice
2 tablespoonfuls Honey
Pinch of Salt
   Shake together with crushed ice.

HONG KONG SPECIAL

½ Gin
¼ Crème de Cacao
¼ Cream

KNOCKOUT

⅓ Vodka
⅓ Absinthe
⅓ Calvados
3 dashes Orange Bitters

MAIDEN'S BLUSH

1 glass Dry Gin
4 dashes Grenadine
4 dashes Orange Curaçao
1 dash Lemon juice

MAIDEN'S PRAYER

⅜ Dry Gin
⅜ Cointreau

COCKTAILS

⅛ Orange juice
⅛ Lemon juice

MANHATTAN

Sweet

½ Canadian Club or Rye Whisky
½ Italian Vermouth

Dry

½ Canadian Club or Rye Whisky
¼ French Vermouth
¼ Italian Vermouth

MARMALADE

2 tablespoonfuls Cooper's Oxford Marmalade
The juice of a large Lemon
4 glasses of Gin
   Squeeze of orange peel in each glass.

DRY MARTINI

½ Gin
½ French Vermouth
1 dash Orange Bitters

COCKTAILS

MARTINI
Dry

⅔ Dry Gin
⅓ French Vermouth

Sweet

⅔ Dry Gin
⅓ Italian Vermouth

Medium

⅓ Dry Gin
⅓ French Vermouth
⅓ Italian Vermouth

MONKEY GLAND

⅔ Dry Gin
⅓ Orange juice
3 dashes Grenadine
3 dashes Absinthe

ORANGE BLOSSOM

½ Dry Gin
½ Orange juice

PARADISE COCKTAIL

⅓ Gin
⅓ Apricot Brandy
⅓ Orange juice

COCKTAILS

PEGU CLUB

⅔ Dry Gin
⅓ Curaçao
1 teaspoonful Lime juice
1 dash Orange Bitters
1 dash Angostura Bitters

PERFECT

⅓ Dry Gin
⅓ French Vermouth
⅓ Italian Vermouth

PHILADELPHIA

Martini (see p. 32) with a dash of Curaçao.

PICCADILLY

⅔ Dry Gin
⅓ French Vermouth
1 dash Grenadine
1 dash Absinthe

PINK GIN

1 glass Gin
1 dash Angostura Bitters

COCKTAILS

PINK LADY

1 glass Plymouth Gin
1 tablespoonful Grenadine
The white of an Egg

PLANTERS

(1)

½ Rum
½ Orange juice
1 dash Lemon juice

(2)

½ Jamaica Rum
¼ Lemon juice
¼ Syrup

PORT WINE COCKTAIL

1 glass Port Wine
1 dash Brandy
   Stir slightly in ice, and strain. Squeeze orange peel on top.

PUBLIC ENEMY NO. 1

½ fresh Orange juice
½ Gin
½ teaspoonful Passion Fruit juice

COCKTAILS

QUAGLINO'S SPECIAL

⅓ Gin
⅓ French Vermouth
⅙ Italian Vermouth
⅙ Grand Marnier
Squeeze of orange peel

QUELLE VIE

⅔ Brandy
⅓ Kümmel

RAINBOW

Make in a liqueur-glass, and pour each ingredient in carefully so that each layer is quite separate and does not mix with the next: *one-seventh each* of:

Crème de Cacao
Crème de Violette
Yellow Chartreuse
Maraschino
Bénédictine
Green Chartreuse
Brandy

An amusing experiment in legerdemain, if nothing more.

COCKTAILS

ROB ROY

½ Scotch Whisky
½ Italian Vermouth
1 dash Angostura Bitters

ROSE (I)

½ Dry Gin
¼ Apricot Brandy
¼ French Vermouth
4 dashes Grenadine
1 dash Lemon juice

ROSE (II)

½ Dry Gin
¼ Kirsch
¼ Cherry Brandy

ROYAL ROMANCE

½ Gin
¼ Grand Marnier
¼ Passion Fruit juice
1 dash Grenadine

SATAN'S WHISKERS
Straight

2 Gin
2 Orange juice

COCKTAILS

2 French Vermouth
2 Italian Vermouth.
1 Grand Marnier
1 dash Orange Bitters

Curled

As above, substituting Orange Curaçao for Grand Marnier.

SAUCY SUE

½ Brandy
½ Calvados
1 dash Apricot Brandy
1 dash Absinthe
    Squeeze orange peel on top.

SCARLET LADY

5 Peach Brandy
3½ Cointreau
2 Gin
1½ Passion Fruit juice

SELF-STARTER

½ Dry Gin
⅜ Lillet
⅛ Apricot Brandy
2 dashes Absinthe

COCKTAILS

SHERRY

1 glass Sherry
4 dashes French Vermouth
4 dashes Orange Bitters

SHERRY AND BITTERS

1 glass medium Sherry
Orange Bitters to taste

SIDECAR

½ Brandy
¼ Cointreau
¼ Lemon juice

SLOE GIN

½ Sloe Gin
¼ French Vermouth
¼ Italian Vermouth

THUNDER AND LIGHTNING

1 glass Brandy
1 Egg yolk
1 teaspoonful powdered Sugar
  Shake, pour out and serve with a dash of
Cayenne pepper on top.

COCKTAILS

TOMATO COCKTAIL

1 tin Tomato juice
1 glass Sherry
1 dessertspoonful Worcester Sauce
Juice of 1 Lemon
1 dessertspoonful of Cream

TRINITY

⅓ Dry Gin
⅓ French Vermouth
⅓ Italian Vermouth

TURF CLUB

½ Gin
½ Grapefruit juice, unsweetened
1 dash Orange Bitters
1 dash Bacardi Rum

VERMOUTH

5½ glasses French Vermouth
1 teaspoonful Maraschino
1 teaspoonful Absinthe Bitters

COCKTAILS

WALDORF

⅓ Dry Gin
⅓ Italian Vermouth
⅓ Absinthe
2 dashes Orange Bitters

WHISKY

1 glass Canadian Club Whisky
4 dashes Syrup
1 dash Angostura Bitters

WHITE LADY

½ Dry Gin
¼ Cointreau
¼ Lemon juice

WILL ROGERS

½ cocktail-glass Plymouth Gin
¼ cocktail-glass Orange juice
¼ cocktail-glass French Vermouth
4 dashes Curaçao

COLD DRINKS

COLD DRINKS

ALLAHABAD TANKARD

Mix together a pint bottle of Pale Ale, a bottle of White Wine, and a quarter of a pint of Syrup. Cut a slice of toast to a round to fit the bottom of a silver tankard, sprinkle on it a quarter of a teaspoonful of Nutmeg and pour over the Ale mixture. Serve with Mint leaves floating on top.

AMERICAN EGG-NOGG

Beat the yolks of four Eggs well, and add to them by degrees a tumblerful and a half of good Brandy, stirring all the time. Then add a pint of rich Cream, four ounces of Castor Sugar and lastly the stiffly whisked whites of the Eggs. Whisk all well together, and set aside for eight hours before drinking.

AMERICAN GLORY

Put the juice of half an Orange into a tumbler,

COLD DRINKS

add two lumps of ice and equal parts of Champagne and Soda Water. Stir and serve.

AMERICAN LEMONADE

Lemon Squash with a quarter gill of Port added on top.

APRICOT COOLER

1 liqueur-glass Apricot Brandy
2 dashes Grenadine
Juice of half a Lemon or one Lime
Fill up with Soda Water

ASSES' MILK

A tot of Rum in a bottle of Lemonade

A SUMMER BEVERAGE

A bottle of Madeira
The thin rind of one Lemon and its juice
Nutmeg and Sugar to taste
Pour over all three quarts of boiling water, and when cold you may strain it and bottle it and, if you like, add a few fresh Tarragon leaves.

44

COLD DRINKS

AULD MAN'S MILK (MEG DODS)

Beat the yolks of six Eggs, and the whites separately. Put to the beaten yolks Sugar and a quart of new Milk or thin sweet Cream. Add to this Rum, Whisky, or Brandy to taste (about a half-pint). Slip in the whipped whites, and give the whole a gentle stir up in the china punch-bowl, in which it should be mixed. It may be flavoured with Nutmeg or Lemon zest. This morning dram is the same as the Egg-nogg of America.

AUTOMOBILE COOLER

1 glass Gin
1 pint Ginger Ale
1 good sprig Mint
A large piece of Ice

BADMINTON

1 bottle of Claret
1 bottle of Soda Water
1 tablespoonful of powdered Sugar
  Serve well iced.

BARBADOES SWIZZLE

$\frac{1}{3}$ Brandy
$\frac{1}{3}$ Cointreau

45

COLD DRINKS

⅓ Lemon juice
1 teaspoonful Sugar
    Shake well with ice.

BLACK VELVET

½ Guinness
½ Champagne

BOSOM CARESSER

Fill shaker half-full of broken ice and add the
yolk of an Egg and a quarter of a gill each of
Madeira, Brandy, Curaçao and Grenadine.

BOSTON COOLER

1 glass Rum
1 dessertspoonful powdered Sugar
Juice of half a Lemon
1 pint of Soda Water

BRANDY SHAKE

Shake well together:
1 tablespoonful Sugar
1 glass Brandy
The juice of two Limes
    Strain into a small glass.

46

COLD DRINKS

BRANDY-SMASH (FRANCATELLI)

Put three slices of Lemon in a tumbler with a
few slices of Pineapple, add a dessertspoonful of
sifted Sugar, fill up with shaved ice; add a wineglass of Brandy; mix and drink devoutly.

BULL-DOG

2 or 3 lumps of Sugar
The juice of an Orange
1 glass of Gin
    Fill up with Ginger Ale.

BULL'S MILK

In a large tumbler mix a teaspoonful of Sugar,
half a pint of Milk, a wineglassful of Brandy, and
half a wineglassful of Rum. Add ice, shake well,
strain, and powder with Cinnamon and Nutmeg.

CHAMPAGNE COBBLER

Put into a tumbler a tablespoonful of Castor
Sugar and a thin paring of Orange and Lemon
peel. Fill up the tumbler two-thirds of the way
with crushed ice, and the remainder with Champagne. Shake and decorate with a slice of Lemon
and one or two small Strawberries, if in season.

COLD DRINKS

CHING-CHING (FRANCATELLI)

A gill of Rum
A sliced Orange
A few drops of Essence of Cloves
4 lumps of Sugar
A tumblerful of shaved ice

CIDER EGG-NOGG

To one beaten Egg slightly sweetened with Sugar allow one glass of Cider. Sprinkle with grated Nutmeg and serve with shaved ice.

Or serve hot.

CIDER POSSET

Pound the peel of a Lemon in a mortar, and pour on to it a quart of Draught Cider. Sweeten to your taste, and then add a gill of Brandy and a quart of Milk. Stir well, and strain through a hair sieve. Serve with Nutmeg grated on it.

CLARET LEMONADE

Dissolve three-quarters of a breakfastcupful of powdered Sugar in the juice of four Lemons and add to it a pint of Claret. Keep on ice, and just before serving add a pint and a half of Soda Water.

48

COLD DRINKS

CLOUDY SKY

A Sloe Gin Rickey (see p. 63), using Ginger Ale instead of Soda Water.

COCA-COLA HIGHBALL

Put into a whisky tumbler:

1 oz. Bourbon Whisky
½ fresh Lemon juice
2 ice cubes
1 teaspoonful Castor Sugar

Stir thoroughly to dissolve the Sugar, and then add:

1 bottle iced Coca-Cola

Drop three leaves of Mint into the tumbler, and bruise them slightly while stirring slowly two or three times.

THE COLLINS FAMILY
Tom Collins

1 glass Dry Gin
½ tablespoonful powdered Sugar
Juice of half a Lemon

Shake and strain into long glass, add lump of ice and split Soda Water.

COLD DRINKS

John Collins: substitute Hollands for Dry Gin.
Rye Collins: substitute Rye Whisky.
Scotch Collins: substitute Scotch Whisky.
Irish Collins: substitute Irish Whisky
Rum Collins: substitute Rum.
Brandy Collins: substitute Brandy.

COUNTRY CLUB COOLER

½ glass Grenadine
½ glass French Vermouth
1 pint Soda Water
1 cube ice

EAU DE FRAISES

You will want a pound of ripe and perfect Strawberries, as any badness will impart an unpleasant flavour to the drink. Put into a stewpan, enamelled, copper, or aluminium (but on no account tinned) three and a half pints of water and three-quarters of a pound of lump Sugar. Let the Sugar dissolve by the side of the fire. Then bring the liquid quickly to the boil, and as soon as it boils, draw the pan from the fire and at once put in the Strawberries. Put on the lid and let them infuse for a good hour. Then strain them through a fine cloth, without pressing them at all, put the liquid on ice, and drink it when it is ready. If you are wise, you will first put in the glasses, when you pour it out, either a little Champagne, or still less Claret, or perhaps best of all a few drops of Kirsch. It is extremely pleasing, but it must be very cold or it may cloy a little.

EGG AND BRANDY DRINK

Get half a dozen brown-shelled very fresh Eggs, wipe them and put them into a glass jar with a stopper, being careful to see that they are not in the least cracked. Squeeze over them the juice of three Lemons, put the stopper in and leave for three days when the eggs will be quite dissolved. Add a quarter of a pound of brown Sugar, and shake until this is dissolved too. Now strain and pour on to half a pint of Brandy. Bottle and keep for a month before using.

ETON BLAZER

¾ Plymouth Gin
¼ Kirsch
½ tablespoonful powdered Sugar
The juice of half a Lemon
Shake and strain into long tumbler, filling up with Soda Water.

COLD DRINKS

FLOSTER

1 gill pale Sherry
½ gill Noyau
6 Peach leaves
3 slices of Lemon
1 oz. Sugar
1 piece of ice
1 bottle iced Soda Water

GIMLET

⅓ Lime Juice Cordial
⅔ Gin
   Shake and fill up with Soda Water.

GIN AND BEER

If Beer in volume is too much for your capacity, a tot of Gin in the next pint will be found helpful.

GIN AND COCA-COLA

Gin
Juice of quarter of a Lemon
1 bottle of Coca-Cola (iced)
   and not at all bad.

COLD DRINKS

GIN AND GINGER ALE
GIN AND GINGER BEER

1 tot Gin
1 bottle Ginger Ale or Ginger Beer
1 large piece of ice

GIN RICKEY

Pour into a tall glass:
1 Port-wineglassful of Gin
The juice of a fresh Lime

Sweeten to taste and fill up with shaved ice. Add a strip of finely pared Lime peel, and fill up with Soda Water.

GIN-SLING (FRANCATELLI)

'Put two slices of Lemon and three lumps of loaf Sugar into a tumbler, fill up to the brim with shaved ice; add a wineglassful of old Gin; stir, and suck through a straw.

'NOTE.—I am afraid that very genteel persons will be exceedingly shocked at the words 'suck through a straw', but when I tell them that the very act of imbibition through a straw prevents the gluttonous absorption of large and baneful quantities of drink, they will, I make no doubt, accept the vulgar precept for the sake of its protection against sudden inebriety.'

COLD DRINKS

GIN SLING

1 Sherry-glassful of fresh Lime juice
2 Sherry-glasses of Dry Gin
1 Sherry-glassful of Cherry Brandy
1 dash of Cointreau
1 bottle Soda Water, and plenty of ice

HAVELOCK

1 gill Ginger Wine
½ gill Brandy
1 lump of ice

HORSE'S NECK (STIFF)

Place the peel of a Lemon in a tumbler with one
end hanging over the top of the glass, add two
lumps of broken ice, a dash of Angostura Bitters,
half a gill of Gin, Brandy, Whisky, etc. as desired,
and fill up with cold Ginger Ale.

ICED COFFEE VARIANT

Add a dessertspoonful of Rum to a tumbler of
the iced Coffee.

IMPERIAL

Boil for twelve minutes an ounce of Cream of
Tartar with half a pound of loaf Sugar in a gallon

COLD DRINKS

of water. Then add the thin rind of a Lemon and the juice of two. Leave on the fire three minutes longer (that is a quarter of an hour in all), let it get cold, and add a little Sherry.

JOHN BRIGHT
Pint of Stout and pint of Bitter.

KARDINAL
Rub a pound of lump Sugar on Orange skin and put it into a bowl with the juice of two Oranges, a cupful of Pineapple juice, a bottle of White Wine and half a bottle of Champagne. Ice very well before serving.

KING'S PEG
A large glass of Champagne laced with a liqueur-glass of Brandy.

KNICKERBOCKER (FRANCATELLI)
Mix a shilling's worth of Lemon ice from the confectioner's with half a pint of Madeira and a pint of iced Seltzer-Water.

COLD DRINKS

LEMONADE (I)

Pare very finely the rinds of six Lemons and two Oranges, put them into a basin or other vessel, and pour a quart of boiling water on them. Add their juice, half a pound of Castor Sugar and half a pint of Sherry. Cover the vessel and let it stand all night. In the morning pour on half a pint of boiling Milk and strain it through a jelly-bag.

LEMONADE (II)

Add the rind and juice of six Lemons to three quarts of Milk, and put in also the whites of six Eggs, half a pound of loaf Sugar, and a bottle of White Wine. Mix well together, boil up and strain through a jelly-bag.

LEMONADE (III)

Rub half a pound of lump Sugar on the rinds of four Lemons, so that it absorbs the 'zest' or coloured outside of the rind. Put the Sugar then into a jug and pour over it half a pint of hot water. Dissolve the Sugar by stirring, and add a quart of White Wine. Strain through a jelly-bag and serve very cold.

COLD DRINKS

LONE TREE COOLER

⅔ Dry Gin
⅓ French Vermouth
1 liqueur-glassful Grenadine
Juice of quarter of a Lemon
Juice of one Orange
Fill up with Soda Water

MAHOGANY

⅔ Gin
⅓ Treacle

MAITRANK

Into a bottle of Hock or Moselle, poured out in
a bowl, put a good handful of Woodruff leaves
and a couple of lumps of Sugar. Keep it well iced,
and after about an hour take the Woodruff out.
Float a few fresh leaves of it in the cup when it is
served, and if you like add some Strawberry and
Black Currant leaves, and a slice of Orange in
each glass. But it is best plain, so long as it is
cold.

MINT COOLER

1 glass Scotch Whisky
3 dashes Crème de Menthe
1 lump of ice
Fill up tumbler with Soda Water

COLD DRINKS

A MINT DRINK

Pick a couple of good sprigs of Mint and strip off the leaves. Put these into a jug and on them three tablespoonfuls of Castor Sugar. Pour in just enough water to dissolve the Sugar, add a wineglassful of liqueur Brandy, and fill up with iced water.

MINT JULEP

Put into a large tumbler two and a half tablespoonfuls of water, one tablespoonful of Castor Sugar and two or three sprigs of bruised Mint. Press these into the Sugar and water to extract the flavour, then add two wineglassfuls of good Brandy, fill up with shaved ice, shake well, add a few Strawberries and slices of Orange, and at the last minute shake in a little rum.

MOTHER-IN-LAW

Half old and half Bitter.

MOTHER'S MILK

Half fill a half-pint tumbler with shaven ice, add a teaspoonful of Raspberry syrup and a liqueurglassful of Brandy, fill up with new Milk, shake well, and serve with straws.

COLD DRINKS

NIGHT-CAP

1 liqueur-glassful old Brandy
1 liqueur-glassful Curaçao
1 liqueur-glassful Bénédictine
Blend for a moment, and say your prayers.

PEACH AND HONEY

1 tablespoonful Honey
1 glass Peach Brandy

PINEAPPLE JULEP

Peel, slice, and cut up a ripe Pineapple into a glass bowl, add the juice of two Oranges, a gill of Raspberry syrup, a gill of Maraschino, a gill of old Gin, a bottle of sparkling Moselle and about a pound of shaven ice. Mix and serve.

PLANTER'S BREAKFAST

To two lumps of ice in a tumbler add a Port-wineglassful of Rum. Add a dash of Lemon juice, and fill up with Ginger Ale.

Sounds like a pleasant libel.

COLD DRINKS

POLICHINELLE

½ glass Cassis
⅙ glass Kirsch
Fill up with iced Soda Water and serve with a lump of ice.

This is drunk in France as an aperitif.

PORT AND LEMON

A glass of Port in a bottle of Lemonade.

RAJAH'S PEG

A large glass of Champagne laced with a liqueur-glass of Brandy.

RASPBERRY NECTAR

Mash up a quart of picked Raspberries in a bowl, sweeten them as you like with Castor Sugar, and let them stew gently for ten minutes. Let them get cold, pour over a bottle of sweet White Wine and add the juice of two Oranges. Strain into a jug and use with iced water.

RUM SHAKE

Shake well together:
1 tablespoonful Sugar

COLD DRINKS

1 glass Rum
The juice of two Limes
   Strain into a small glass.

RUSSIAN VELVET

½ Russian Stout
½ Tonic Water
   Add Tonic Water to Stout.

SAINT CHARLES (FRANCATELLI)

A shilling's-worth of Cherry Water ice from the
confectioner's, mixed with a small glass of Kirsch
and a bottle of iced Soda Water.

SHADY GROVE COOLER

1 glass Dry Gin
The juice of half a Lemon
½ tablespoonful Sugar
   Fill up with Ginger Beer.

SHANDY GAFF

Add a lump of ice and a bottle of Ginger Beer
to a pint of Mild or Bitter Ale.

COLD DRINKS

SHERRY AND LEMON

A glass of medium Sherry in a bottle of Lemonade.

SHERRY BLUSH

Put into a small tumbler a wineglassful of Sherry and thirty drops of Raspberry syrup. Fill up with shaved ice, shake, pour out, and decorate with whole Raspberries or Strawberries.

SHERRY COBBLER

Pour into a tumbler two glasses of Sherry and add a tablespoonful of Castor Sugar and two or three slices of Orange. Fill up with crushed ice, shake well, and drink through straws.

A SHERRY DRINK

Mix a bottle of Sherry with two bottles of Ginger Beer.

SHERRY SANGAREE

Put a wineglassful of Sherry with a teaspoonful of Icing Sugar into a small tumbler and fill to one third with shaved ice. Shake, and serve with a dust of Nutmeg.

COLD DRINKS

SIFTER

½ gill Whisky
1 tablespoonful Honey
½ gill Strawberry syrup
A tumbler of shaved ice.

SLEEPY HEAD

1 glass Brandy
1 piece Orange peel
4 leaves fresh Mint
 Fill up with Ginger Ale. In long tumbler.

SLOE GIN RICKEY

Squeeze the juice of half a good-sized Lime into a tumbler containing a lump or two of ice. Add three-quarters of a gill of Sloe Gin, and fill up with cold Soda Water.

SPIDER

Gin and Lemonade, iced.

SPIKE LEMONADE

Whisky and Lemonade: usually Rye Whisky.

COLD DRINKS

STONE FENCE

1 glass Scotch Whisky
2 dashes Angostura Bitters
1 lump of ice
In long tumbler. Fill up with Soda Water.

STRAIGHT SCOTCH HIGHBALL

Put two or three lumps of ice into a tumbler, add three-quarters of a gill of Scotch Whisky, and fill up with cold Soda Water.

In other words, a Whisky-and-Soda.

SUMMER DRINK

Make some moderately strong tea, let it stand for five minutes and then strain it into a jug. Sweeten as you like, add a Lemon thinly sliced, put a cover over the jug and leave it until quite cold. Just before serving add a glass of any kind of liqueur you prefer, and a heaped tablespoonful of crushed ice.

SURGEON-MAJOR

Two Eggs beaten up in a large glass which is filled up with Champagne.

COLD DRINKS

TEWAHDIDDLE (DR. KITCHENER)

A pint of Table Beer (or Ale, if you intend it for a supplement to your 'Night-Cap'), a tablespoonful of Brandy, and a teaspoonful of brown Sugar, or Clarified Syrup—a very little grated Nutmeg or Ginger may be added, and a roll of very thin-cut lemon peel.

TWIST

Half-and-half, Gin and Rum.

UNCLE

Half-and-half, Old and Mild.

VELVET BLUSH

1 wineglass Sauternes
½ wineglass Sherry
A small piece Lemon rind
A little Icing Sugar

Put into a small tumbler, fill up with shaved ice, shake and strain. If possible, decorate with a sprig of Verbena.

HOT DRINKS

HOT DRINKS

ALE POSSET

½ pint of Sherry
½ pint of Burton
A quart of boiling Milk sweetened with a table-spoonful of white Sugar

Mix well, strain, and add grated Nutmeg before serving.

BISHOP (WILLIAM HONE'S YEAR BOOK)

'Make incisions in the rind of a Lemon, stick Cloves in the incisions and roast the Lemon by a slow fire. Put small but equal quantities of Cinnamon, Cloves, Mace, and Allspice and a root of Ginger into a saucepan with half a pint of water; let it boil until it is reduced by half. Boil a bottle of Port Wine, and by applying a lighted paper to the saucepan, burn a portion of the spirit out of it. Add the roasted Lemon and Spice into the Wine; stir all well together, and let it stand near the fire for ten minutes. Put some knobs on the rind of a

69

Lemon' (i.e. rub the rind with some lumps of Sugar) 'put the Sugar into a bowl or jug with the juice of half a Lemon not roasted; pour the Wine upon this mixture, grate Nutmeg into it, sweeten to taste, and you have a "Bishop". Serve it up with the Lemon and Spice floating in it.'

If an Orange is used instead of a lemon it is a London Bishop. The above is an Oxford one.

BISHOP

'It is, as I have found more people not know than know in this ghastly thin-faced time of ours, simply mulled Port. You take a bottle of that noble liquor and put it in a saucepan, adding as much or as little water as you can reconcile to your taste and conscience, an Orange cut in half (I believe some people squeeze it lightly) and plenty of Cloves (you may stick them in the Orange if you have a mind). Sugar or no Sugar at discretion, and with regard to the character of the wine. Put it on the fire, and as soon as it is warm, and begins to steam, light it. The flames will be of an imposingly infernal colour, quite different from the light-blue flicker of spirits or of Claret mulled. Before it has burned too long pour it into a bowl, and drink it as hot as you like. It is an excellent liquor, and I have found it quite popular with ladies.' (Professor Saintsbury.)

HOT DRINKS

BLUE BLAZER

Put into a silver jug or mug, which has first been heated, two wineglassfuls of good Scotch Whisky, and one wineglassful of boiling water. Set the Whisky on fire, and pour the blazing liquid into another heated mug or jug, pouring them back and forth. Serve in a tumbler with a lump of Sugar and a little thinly pared Lemon rind.

BROWN CAUDLE OR THE SCOTS ALEBERRY

Mix two large spoonfuls of finely ground Oatmeal in mild sweet small Beer two hours previous to using it; strain it from the grits and boil it. Sweeten and add Wine and Seasonings to taste. Nutmeg or a little Lemon juice answers best for Seasoning. So writes Meg Dods.

BURNT COFFEE

Make some good strong Coffee, sweeten it rather more than usual, and strain it into small cups. Pour a little Brandy into each over a spoon, set light to it, and when the brandy is partly consumed, blow out the flame and drink the coffee at once.

HOT DRINKS

CHURCHWARDEN

Roast a Lemon before the fire and cut it in quarters, take out the pips and put the quarters into a large tumbler. Add a tablespoonful of fine Sugar, two wineglasses of hot Port Wine and one of hot Tea.

EGG FLIP

Beat up three Eggs with a quarter of a pound of moist Sugar. Heat up a pint and a half of Beer, but it must not come to the boil, then mix it with the Eggs and Sugar gradually and whisking well. When ready, grate a little Nutmeg on top.

GLÖGG

Put a bottle of Brandy into a saucepan with a small piece of Cinnamon, ten Cardamoms, ten Cloves, and a handful each of Raisins and blanched Almonds. Put seven ounces of lump Sugar on a wire tray over the saucepan, set light to the Brandy, and while it burns ladle it over the Sugar until it has all melted. Then put the lid on the pan at once, and just before serving add a wineglassful of Port, Madeira, or Burgundy. Serve hot with a few Almonds and Raisins in each glass.

72

HOT DRINKS

GLÜHWEIN

Put two lumps of Sugar in a saucepan with a slice of Lemon, a piece of Cinnamon and half a pint of Claret. Boil and serve as hot as possible.

HET PINT (MEG DODS)

Grate a Nutmeg into two quarts of Mild Ale, and bring to the point of boiling. Mix a little cold Ale with Sugar as necessary to sweeten this, and three Eggs well beaten. Gradually mix the hot Ale with the Eggs, taking care that they do not curdle. Put in half a pint of Whisky, and bring it once more nearly to the boil, and then briskly pour it from one vessel to another until it becomes smooth and bright.

HOME RULER

Beat up two Egg yolks with a little Sugar, gradually add to them, stirring well, a tumbler of hot milk, and finally add a large wineglassful of John Jameson Whisky.

HONEYSUCKLE

Dissolve two teaspoonfuls of honey in a tumbler with boiling water. Add a slice of Lemon, Rum to your taste or discretion, fill up with hot water and stir well before sampling.

HOT DRINKS

HOT SPICED ALE

Boil a quart of good Ale. Add half a Nutmeg grated. Beat up two Eggs and mix them with a little cold Ale, and when they are ready, add the warm Ale and stir to a froth.

LAMB'S WOOL

Mash eight roasted Apples, moisten with a quart of old Ale, press and strain. Season with powdered Ginger and grated Nutmeg, sweeten to taste; warm up and drink while warm.

LAWN SLEEVES

Take a quarter of a pound of lump Sugar, and rub this on the rind of a Lemon until you have rubbed off all the yellow part. Then add to this two Lemons cut in thin slices, four wineglasses of liquid Calf's Foot Jelly, and a discreet flavouring of Cinnamon, Mace, Cloves, and Allspice. Put these into a jug together and pour over a quart of boiling water. Put a lid on the jug, leave it for a quarter of an hour, and then add a bottle of Sauternes or any sweet wine. Grate a Nutmeg into it, and sweeten further if desired.

HOT DRINKS

LE BRULO

I am indebted to the late Countess Morphy's *Recipes of all Nations* for these two Creole drinks.

1. Pour two wineglasses of good Brandy in a silver bowl, half a wineglassful of Kirsch, the same of Maraschino, and add a pinch of Cinnamon and Allspice. Put in about ten lumps of Sugar, and when they have absorbed the liqueurs, put them in a ladle, cover with Brandy, and set alight. Burn for a few minutes, and serve in wineglasses.

2. Cut a large thick-skinned Orange in half, removing all the pulp and putting two lumps of Sugar in each half Orange. Fill each with Brandy and set alight. After a few minutes pour the Brandy into glasses. Burning it in the Orange gives it a very pleasant flavour.

LOCOMOTIVE

Put two Egg yolks into a goblet, with an ounce of Honey, a little Essence of Cloves, and a liqueur-glass of Curaçao; add a pint of Burgundy made hot, whisk well together, and serve hot in glasses.

MULLED ALE

Put a quart of good Ale into a saucepan, and add a tablespoonful of Sugar, a pinch of ground

Cloves, a pinch of Nutmeg, and a large pinch of ground Ginger. Bring nearly to the boil, and add a wineglassful of Rum or Brandy.

MULLED WINE

Boil three ounces of white Sugar with a wineglass and a half of water and a quarter of an ounce of mixed Spice until it is a syrup, then stir into it a bottle of Claret or Port and bring slowly to the boil. It must just come to boiling point.

NEGUS

Put a pint of Port Wine into a jug, adding four ounces of lump Sugar which have been rubbed on the rind of a Lemon. Add the strained juice of the Lemon, a little grated Nutmeg and a quart of boiling water. Cover, and when cool, drink it.

ANOTHER NEGUS

Mix a teaspoonful of Icing Sugar with two wineglasses of Port, adding a little grated Nutmeg and pounded Cloves. Moisten further with a wineglassful of boiling water and a split of Soda.

HOT DRINKS

NEGUS, WHITE WINE

See LAWN SLEEVES (p. 74).

NIGHT-CAP

Heat up half a pint of old Ale, and just before it boils pour it into a tumbler and add a tablespoonful of moist Sugar, two tablespoonfuls of Brandy and a grating of Nutmeg.

PURL

Heat a pint of Ale and just before it boils take it off the fire and stir in three Egg yolks which have been beaten with two tablespoonfuls of Sugar and a pinch of Ginger and Nutmeg. Add a glass of Gin, and pour backwards and forwards between two heated jugs. Serve it frothing.

SLEEPER

To a gill of old Rum add one ounce of Sugar, two yolks of Eggs and the juice of half a Lemon; boil half a pint of water with six Cloves, six Coriander Seeds, and a bit of Cinnamon, whisk all together and strain them into a tumbler.

HOT DRINKS

UNCLE TOBY

Rub the rind of a Lemon on two lumps of Sugar. Put the Sugar into a large tumbler with the juice of the Lemon, and pour over a wineglassful of boiling water to dissolve it. Add a wineglassful of Brandy, a wineglassful of Rum, and two wineglassfuls of hot Stout. Mix well, and strain. Sweeten further if desired.

VIN CHAUD

Sweeten a bottle of Claret or Burgundy to your taste, and heat it up slowly in a pan with a stick of Cinnamon. As soon as it approaches boiling point (for on no account must it actually boil), take it off the fire, remove the Cinnamon stick, and serve the hot wine in glasses in the bottom of which there is already a slice of Lemon.

WASSAIL BOWL

To a quart of hot Ale add a quarter of an ounce each of grated Nutmeg, powdered Ginger and Cinnamon, half a bottle of Sherry, two slices of toast, the juice and peel of a Lemon and two baked Apples. Sweeten to taste.

HOT DRINKS

WHISKY TODDY

Pour boiling water slowly into a tumbler until it is about half full, and leave it there until the glass is thoroughly heated. Then pour it away, and put in a wineglassful of boiling water with Sugar to taste. When the Sugar is melted, add half a glass of Whisky, stir with a silver spoon, add more boiling water, then another half-glass of Whisky, and stir and serve hot.

CUPS

CUPS

ALE CUP

Add to three pints of mild Ale the juice of a Lemon, a tablespoonful of Sugar, a glass of Sherry, some grated Nutmeg, and a sprig of Mint.

ALE CUP (JOHN'S NECTAR)

Grate some Ginger into a quart tankard, add a wineglassful of Gin and Bitters, then a pint of good hot Ale, and drink while frothing.

A MIXED CUP

Put a bottle of Claret in a decanter, and pour into it a bottle of Hock, adding a spoonful of Sugar and a slice of Lemon. Also add the very thinly pared rind of a Lemon, but only let it stay there for ten minutes. Ice before serving with or without the addition of Soda Water.

CUPS

APRICOT CUP

1 bottle Burgundy
1 liqueur-glassful Apricot Brandy
1 liqueur-glassful Curaçao
½ bottle Soda Water
A few Mint leaves, Strawberries and slices of Apricot.

BACCHUS CUP

½ bottle Champagne
½ pint Sherry
⅛ pint Brandy
1 liqueur-glass Noyeau
1 tablespoonful Castor Sugar
1 bottle Soda Water
A few leaves of Balm
Ice

BEER CUP

1 quart of Ale
1 glass of Brandy
1 spoonful of brown Sugar
The peel of a Lemon
A few slices of Apple
A little Nutmeg
Some sprigs of Borage and, if possible, Burnet.

CUPS

BULL'S-EYE CUP

1 pint Ginger Ale
1 pint sparkling Cider
1 liqueur-glassful Brandy

BURGUNDY CUP

1 bottle Burgundy
½ bottle Port
2 bottles Soda Water
1 liqueur-glassful Chartreuse
The juice of two Oranges
The juice of one Lemon
A few thin slices of Cucumber, one or two sprigs
of fresh Lemon Thyme
1 tablespoonful Castor Sugar

Mix all the ingredients except the Port, and leave them covered closely on ice for an hour. Add the Port just before serving.

CHAMPAGNE CUP

1 bottle of Champagne
1 liqueur-glassful of Brandy
1 liqueur-glassful of Curaçao
A siphon of Soda Water

Decorate with different sorts of fruit in season, and a sprig of fresh Mint or Borage.

CUPS

CHAMPAGNE CUP (SIMPLE)

2 bottles Champagne
½ pint Strawberry or Lemon Water ice
2 bottles Soda Water
    Mix and serve at once. See that the Champagne
and the Soda Water is well iced.

CIDER CUP (I)

Enough for four. A liqueur-glassful of Calvados or Apple Jack, the same of ordinary
Brandy, the same of Curaçao, a bottle of Cider,
two or three nice pieces of ice, and a frothing of
Soda Water.

CIDER CUP (II)

1 quart Cider
A small glass of Sherry
A little Maraschino
A small glass of Brandy
3 slices of Lemon
1 Orange sliced
A sprig of Borage
2 bottles of Soda Water

CIDER CUP (III)

Pass through a sieve half a dozen baked Apples,

86

pour over the purée a pint of boiling water, and leave it all night. The next day strain it, add some Lemon slices, a bottle of Raspberry Cordial, and put on the ice. When serving, add a bottle of Lemonade.

CLARET CUP (I)

Put into a jug an ounce of lump Sugar, the rind of an Orange and of a Lemon, three thin slices of each of these with the pips removed, a strip of Cucumber peel, a tablespoonful of Angostura Bitters, and a liqueur-glassful each of Brandy, Curaçao and Maraschino. Add a bottle and a half of Claret and as much Soda Water as you think fit. Let this mixture infuse for a little while with the jug covered, then strain and put in a few pieces of ice and some leaves of freshly picked Mint.

CLARET CUP (II)

Slice an Orange and half a Lemon and put them into a basin or jug with some pieces of Sugar Candy, a sprig of Mint, a little Cucumber rind, and as much Brandy and Curaçao (twice as much Brandy as Curaçao) as you like, or can afford. Leave this covered for at least a couple of hours, then add two bottles of Claret. Keep on ice until wanted, then complete with a siphon of Soda Water. You can add a little Sugar if you like, but it must be done before the Soda Water is added.

CLARET CUP (III)

Stone and crush up a pint of Cherries, the blacker and riper the better, and add the juice of three Lemons and of one Orange and a breakfast-cupful of Castor Sugar. Leave to stand for five or six hours, then strain it and add a pint of Claret and a quart of Soda Water.

CLARET CUP (NATHANIEL GUBBINS)

2 bottles Pontet Canet
2 wineglasses old Brandy
1 wineglass Curaçao
1 pint bottle sparkling Moselle
2 bottles Soda Water
A sprig or two of Borage and a little Lemon peel
Sugar *ad lib*

Add the Moselle and Soda Water just before using.

CLARET CUP (AUSTRIAN)

Soak a pound of crushed, stoned, Black Cherries in a quarter of a bottle of Rum for several hours in a cool place. Then add two or three bottles of Claret, a sliced Orange, some thinly cut Lemon peel and a few sprigs of Borage. Ice well and add Soda Water.

CLARET CUP (PROFESSOR SAINTSBURY)

In his own words:

'Instead of Soda Water I used sparkling Moselle, in the proportion of a pint of this to a bottle of Claret, with thick slices of Pineapple instead of Lemon and one big lump of ice as big as a baby's head. It was astonishing how the people lapped it up. . . .'

And I don't blame them. It is as delicious as it sounds and I can say *'Bu et approuvé'*. But the Pineapple must of course be a fresh one.

CLUB CUP

1 wineglassful Canadian Club Whisky
The juice of a Lemon
1 bottle Ginger Ale

ESKRICK PARK CIDER CUP (MRS. ROUNDELL)

First take the peel of a Lemon, twelve lumps of Sugar and a little water. Boil to a syrup, so as to extract the flavour of the peel. Then put into a jug some sprigs of Borage, some slices of Cucumber and of Lemon and a little grated Nutmeg. Add a pint of Sherry, a bottle of Cider, one glass of Ale, and a bottle of Soda Water. Sweeten with syrup according to your taste. To make two quarts of Cup.

HOCK CUP (I)

Mix a couple of liqueur-glassfuls of Maraschino with one of Curaçao; sweeten with a dessert-spoonful of Sugar; fill up with a bottle of Hock. Decorate with slices of Orange, add a small piece of Cucumber peel, and if you like, float a few Mint leaves on top.

Sauternes can be used in the same way.

HOCK CUP (II)

1 bottle Hock
1 glass Bénédictine
1 glass Brandy
1 liqueur-glass Curaçao
1 glass Yellow Chartreuse
Some slices of Cucumber and Lemon
A sprig of Borage
A large lump of ice

1½ bottles of Soda Water

Leave to stand for a few minutes, then remove the Lemon and Cucumber slices and add a few fresh ripe Strawberries.

HOCK CUP (III)

1 bottle Dry Hock
2 tots Brandy
2 tots Curaçao
A splash of Soda Water
Add ice, Grapes cut in half, slices of Orange, Lemon, Banana, and Apple, and a sprig or two of Borage.

INSTITUTION CUP

A pint of Champagne
A gill of Pineapple syrup
A gill of Strawberry syrup
An Orange cut in slices
A glass of Brandy
A tumbler of shaved ice
Shake together and strain into tumblers.

KING CUP (MRS. ROUNDELL)

Take the thinly pared rind of a Lemon and all its juice, a small piece of bruised Ginger and two

CUPS

lumps of Sugar. Pour a pint and a half of boiling water over them, and let it stand to get cold. When quite cold, stir in a glass of Sherry.

LIQUEUR CUP

1 pint Claret
1 pint Water
1 tablespoonful Maraschino
1 tablespoonful Kirsch or Brandy
1 thinly sliced Orange
The juice of two Oranges and three Lemons
1 tablespoonful Castor Sugar
Broken ice

LOVING CUP

Rub the peel of one Lemon with some lumps of Sugar, then peel that Lemon and another so that there is not a vestige of pith left, and cut the fruit into thin slices. Put these, with a few leaves of Balm and a sprig of Borage into a jug with the Lemon Sugar and add a pint and a half of water, half a bottle of Madeira and a quarter of a pint of Brandy. Cover and put on ice for an hour. Then just when about to serve add a bottle of iced Champagne.

CUPS

MERTON COLLEGE CIDER CUP

To one quart of Cider add two wineglasses of Sherry and one of Brandy, a little Nutmeg, and a few slices of Lemon. Sweeten with Sugar. Serve up with a little ice and sprigs of Balm and Borage. Do not leave the herbs in too long.

MINT CUP

Pare three Lemons very thinly. Put the rind into a jug with the juice, add two sprigs of Mint and three ounces of lump Sugar, and pour over two and half pints of boiling water. Cover and leave until cold, then strain and add a glass of Sherry. Serve very cold.

MOSELLE CUP

1 bottle Moselle
1 glass Brandy
4 or 5 thin slices Pineapple
The peel of half a Lemon cut very thin
Ice, and Sugar, *ad lib*.

Just before using add a bottle of Soda Water.

PEACH CUP

Prick all over with a silver fork one ripe,

skinned Peach for each person. Put each into a large tall goblet and fill up with iced Hock or Moselle.

PEACH CUP (ADALOR CUP)

Prick a large ripe Peach all over with a silver fork, and put it in a pint of Champagne.

PORT WINE CUP

Heat up until warm half a pint of Port with two ounces of Sugar and a little Spice. Strain clear, and when cold add a bottle of Soda Water.

RED CURRANT CUP

Make a syrup of a pint of water and a pound of Sugar. When it is cool, pour it over some stalked Currants, leave on ice for four hours, and serve.

SHERRY CUP (1)

2 bottles Sherry
½ pint Cognac
¼ pint Curaçao

CUPS

3 drops Essence of Almonds
Mix well, ice and add a slice of Cucumber and three or four bottles of Soda Water.

SHERRY CUP (II)

1 bottle Sherry
2 bottles Soda Water
2 bottles Schweppes Lemonade
1 liqueur-glassful of Curaçao poured into a wine-glass and filled up with Brandy
   Ice well.

SHERRY CUP

'A very little fizzing water, a good dose of stout, well-flavoured Sherry, just a *pousse* of Brandy, with Lemon and Borage, will make *the* drink for hot weather. . . .' (Professor Saintsbury.)

STRAWBERRY CUP

Put a pound of Strawberries, wild ones being best, into a bowl with half a pound of Castor Sugar and leave them for an hour. Then add three bottles of Hock, and put the mixture on ice. Before serving add a bottle of iced Champagne, and serve with a few of the Strawberries in each glass.

CUPS

1 pint Dry Champagne
1 pint Claret
1 large piece of ice
Decorate with fruit and sprigs of Mint.

PUNCHES

PUNCHES

BARBADOES PUNCH

1 tablespoonful Raspberry syrup
1 tablespoonful Castor Sugar
1 wineglass of Water
2 wineglasses of Brandy
½ a wineglassful of Guava jelly
The juice of half a Lemon
2 slices of Orange
1 slice of Pineapple
  Ice and shake well.

CHERRY PUNCH

Stone and mash up a pound of Cherries and put them into a bowl with the juice of three Lemons and two Oranges and a slice or two of Pineapple. Cover with a pint of Sugar and leave for an hour. Now press and strain, heat up the liquid and when it is cold again, add a quart each of Soda Water and Claret and four ounces of very ripe Cherries.

PUNCHES

CIDER PUNCH

Bring to the boil a quart of Cider, with a few lumps of Sugar and three Oranges stuck with Cloves, and let it boil for two or three minutes. Now add a good glass of Whisky, and pour the whole thing into a bowl, from which you must serve it very hot.

DEVIL'S CUP PUNCH

1 liqueur-glass Green Chartreuse
1 liqueur-glass Yellow Chartreuse
1 liqueur-glass Bénédictine
2 liqueur-glasses Brandy
2 quarts iced Champagne

FISH HOUSE PUNCH

To be made in proportion. These are eighteenth-century quantities!

Mix together some time before using:

4 quarts water
1 quart Jamaica Rum
1 tumbler Brandy
1 glass of Curaçao
1 pint Lemon juice
½ tumbler Peach Brandy
1 shredded Pineapple

PUNCHES

The juice of two Oranges
2 sliced Lemons
   Sweeten to taste.
   About an hour before serving, add a large piece of ice and a bottle of iced Champagne.

GIN PUNCH

Peel a Lemon, pour half a pint of Gin on it (the peel), add the juice and a little Sugar, a pint of water, a glass of Maraschino, and two bottles of iced Soda Water.

GLASGOW PUNCH

Put into a tumbler a tablespoonful of Icing Sugar, the juice of a Lemon, and a wineglassful of Jamaica Rum. Fill the glass with chipped ice, and stir well.

LAGER BEER PUNCH

Pare a Lemon finely, and put the strips into a jug with a small cupful of water, a glass of Sherry, the juice of two Lemons, a pinch of grated Nutmeg, a tablespoonful of Castor Sugar, and a few leaves of Mint. Put a cover over it and let it stand for about twenty minutes. Then strain it and add to it a bottle of Lager Beer and a good number of pieces of ice.

PUNCHES

MARQUISE PUNCH

Heat a bottle of Sauternes with half a pound of Sugar, the peel of a Lemon and two Cloves. As soon as a white froth appears on the surface of the wine, take the pan off the fire and add a glass of warmed Brandy. Set light to it. When the flames have died down, remove the Lemon peel and Cloves, and serve the punch in glasses with a slice of Lemon in each.

MILK PUNCH
(To drink with Turtle Soup)

Prepare a syrup from half a pint of water and three and a half ounces of Sugar, the consistence being 17 (Baumé's Hydrometer). Set to infuse in this syrup two Orange and two Lemon *zests* (that is, the coloured part only of the peel). Strain at the end of ten minutes, and add half a pint of Rum, a fifth of a pint of Kirsch, two-thirds of a pint of Milk, and the juice of three Oranges and three Lemons. Mix thoroughly. Let it stand for three hours; filter and serve cold.

(From Escoffier's *Guide to Modern Cookery*.)

FRESH MINT PUNCH

With a wooden spoon crush the leaves from half a dozen sprigs of Mint, then squeeze over them the juice of three Lemons and six Oranges, adding six ounces of Castor Sugar. Stir these well together, then pour them over a lump of ice in a bowl, adding three pints of Ginger Ale and one of Cider.

NORFOLK PUNCH

Peel six Lemons and three Seville Oranges very thinly, squeeze the juice into a large jug, and pour in two quarts of Brandy and one of White Wine. Add a quart of Milk and a pound and a quarter of Sugar, mix well and leave for twenty-four hours. Then run it through a jelly-bag, and bottle it.

OLD ENGLISH PUNCH

Rub the rind of a Lemon on a quarter of a pound of lump Sugar. Dissolve the Sugar in boiling water, then add half a pint of boiling Ale, a gill of strong hot Tea, the juice of a Lemon and a wineglassful each of Brandy and Rum.

PEACH PUNCH

Peel, stone, and cut in slices a dozen ripe Peaches. Put them in a bowl and sprinkle them with plenty of Sugar. Leave them there for a couple of hours and then pour over them a bottle of Red Wine and a bottle of White Wine. See that they are well iced, and just before serving add a bottle of iced Champagne.

PFIRSICHBOWLE (PEACH PUNCH)

Peel, stone, and slice a dozen ripe Peaches. Put them in a bowl, sprinkle them with plenty of Sugar, and let them stand for a couple of hours. Then pour over them a bottle of Red Wine and a bottle of White Wine. Ice well, and just before serving add a bottle of iced Champagne.

PUNCH WITH KIRSCH

Throw a good half-ounce of Tea, says Escoffier, into one quart of boiling water, and let it infuse for ten minutes. Put into a punch or salad bowl one pound of loaf Sugar; strain the infusion of Tea over the Sugar, and dissolve the latter, stirring the while with a wooden spoon. Add one and a half pints of Kirsch, set it alight, and serve in glasses.

Lesser quantities in proportion, of course.

PUNCHES

RUM PUNCH (PROFESSOR SAINTSBURY)

'The recipe . . . for real punch is as follows: three parts Rum, two of Brandy, one of Lemon juice, and six of hot water, the quantity of Sugar being a matter quite of taste. I never knew this mixture found fault with by respectable persons of any age, sex or condition, from undergraduates to old ladies, at any hour between sunset and sunrise.' (*Notes from a Cellar Book.*)

RUM PUNCH

Put half a pound of powdered Sugar into a bowl with the rind of a Lemon and half a pint of water. Let it dissolve, then add a bottle of Rum, a bottle of White Wine, a Lemon squeezed, and two liqueur-glassfuls of Curaçao. Serve with pieces of broken ice in the jug.

SUMMER PUNCH

Pour half a pint of Gin on the thinly pared rind of a Lemon and squeeze in the juice of half a Lemon. Then add a glass of Maraschino, a pint and a quarter of cold water and two bottles of iced Soda Water. Do not ice the Punch: it is better to have the Soda Water well iced.

PUNCHES

SWEDISH PUNSCH

4½ quarts Water
13 lb. Preserving Sugar
7½ whole bottles best Arrack
¼ bottle Whisky
½ bottle dark Sherry

Boil water and Sugar for two minutes in preserving-pan. Skim well. When cold, stir in Arrack, Whisky, and Sherry. Keep on ladling the Punsch for quite an hour. Bottle, cork and seal bottle, and keep in lying position. Improved with time, but can be used after two days. (From *Good Food from Sweden*, by Inga Norberg.)

LIQUEURS

Liqueurs are admirable for those who like them. They are also delicious as flavours: *Grand Marnier* or *Bénédictine* with Strawberries, *Kirsch* with Cherries and Peaches, *Kümmel* sometimes with Apple, as in *Pommes Moscovite*. But when it comes to the end of a meal, then say I, with my friend Charles Walter Berry, 'I'd rather have Brandy.'

A short list of
LIQUEURS
which are generally to be purchased

Abricotine
Advocaat
Amourette
Angelica
Anisette
Apple Brandy
Apple Gin
Apple Jack
Apricot Brandy
Apricot Gin
Aurum
Banane de la Martinique
Bénédictine
Blackberry Brandy
Bullace Gin
Calvados
Capricot
Cassis
Cerasella
Chartreuse, Yellow

Chartreuse, Green
Cherry Brandy
Cherry Gin
Cherry Whisky
Cointreau
Cordial Médoc
Crème de Bananes
Crème de Cacao
Crème de Cassis
Crème de Chocolat
Crème de Cumin
Crème de Mandarine
Crème de Menthe
Crème de Moka
Crème de Noyau
Crème de Prunelles
Crème de Roses
Crème de Thé
Crème de Vanille
Crème de Violettes

LIQUEURS

Curaçao

Damson Gin

Drambuie

Fraisia

Ginger Brandy

Ginger Whisky

Goldwasser

Grand Marnier

Half Om Half

Kirschwasser

Kümmel

Liqueur d'Or

Mandarin

Mandarine

Maraschino

Monastine

Noyau

Orange Brandy

Parfait Amour

Peach Brandy

Pécheuse

Prunelle

Quetsch

Rabinovka

Raspail

Ratafia

Sloe Gin

Strega

Tangerinette

Van der Hum

Vieille Cure

HOME-MADE DRINKS

HOME-MADE DRINKS

ATHOLE BROSE

Put a pound of Honey into a basin and add about a teacupful of water, so that the Honey dissolves. Stir it with a silver spoon and when well mixed add gradually one and a half pints of Whisky. Stir briskly until a froth begins to rise, then bottle and keep tightly corked.

BIRCH WINE

To every gallon of Birch juice, add four pounds of granulated Sugar, two Nutmegs, and the thin peel of a Lemon. Boil and skim this well, and clarify with whites and shell of Egg. When cool, put fresh Yeast to it and let it ferment for two days. Season with Essence of Almonds. Then close up the cask, cement it with lime and leave it thus for six weeks. Then bottle.

HOME-MADE DRINKS

BLACKBERRY BRANDY

Mix equal parts of Blackberry juice and Brandy, and for each gallon of the mixture allow one pound of loaf Sugar.

BLACKBERRY CORDIAL

1 quart Blackberry juice
1 lb. lump Sugar
1 oz. stick Cinnamon
1 oz. whole Allspice
1 oz. whole Nutmegs
1 oz. whole Cloves

Tie the Spices in a clean cloth, boil all together for half an hour, and then skim well. Bottle while hot, and seal down. To drink, dilute with cold water.

BLACKBERRY VINEGAR

Put two pounds of Blackberries into a basin, press them gently with a wooden spoon, pour over a quart of White Wine Vinegar, cover the basin with a cloth and leave it for twenty-four hours. Next day put another two pounds of Blackberries in another basin, and strain on to them the liquid from the first basin. Cover and leave again for twenty-four hours. On the third day, do the same, and on the fourth strain the liquid into a preserving-pan. Dissolve in it a pound of Sugar for every pint of the liquid, then boil for a quarter of an hour, skim, and bottle. Use with water or Soda Water, like Raspberry Vinegar.

BLACK CURRANT CORDIAL

In a large earthenware jar put alternate layers of Black Currants and Demerara Sugar, and a dozen or so crushed Cloves in a muslin bag, using equal quantities of fruit and sugar. Cover completely airtight (this must be done), and leave for six weeks, then strain off the syrup and for each six pounds of berries and sugar used add a large glassful of Brandy. Mix well, put into bottles and cork them well.

BRAMBLE TIP WINE

Nip off about an inch from the end of the tips of Bramble shoots, and when you have a gallon, measure them, boil them in a gallon of water with four pounds of Sugar for an hour. Strain this liquid, let it stand and ferment for about a fortnight, then strain it again and bottle it.

HOME-MADE DRINKS

CHERRY BOUNCE

Stone twelve pounds of Cherries, put the fruit in a large jar and stand this in a saucepan of boiling water. Cook gently until all the juice is extracted, then strain and measure it into a preserving-pan. Now for each gallon of juice add four pounds of Sugar, half a teaspoonful of ground Mace and a quarter of a teaspoonful of ground Allspice. Simmer until the scum ceases to rise, skim and when cold add, for each gallon, a quart of Brandy and a quart of Rum. Bottle.

CHERRY BRANDY

'Weigh fine Morellas, cut off half the stalk, prick them with a needle, drop them in a glass or wide-mouthed bottle, pound three-quarters the weight of loaf Sugar, strew it over them, and fill up with Brandy. Tie a bladder over.'

CHERRY CORDIAL

Take a gallon of strained Cherry juice, add two pounds of Sugar and boil for half an hour. Add half a pint of Brandy, and when it is cold, bottle it.

CHERRY WINE

Put three pounds of Morella Cherries into an

earthenware jar, sprinkle them with three pounds of Sugar and add a quart of old Ale. Cork down and leave for at least six months, then strain and bottle.

CIDER

For this you must use six pounds of Apples and two to two and a half pounds of Sugar to each gallon of water. Wash and quarter the Apples without peeling them. Cover them with the water and stir, and occasionally crush them, every day for three weeks. Then strain them through a colander. Add Sugar to the liquid and leave for three or four days, stirring now and again. Strain through a jelly-bag, and having bottled it leave it for at least three weeks.

CLOVE BRANDY

Bruise two ounces of Cloves and two ounces of Coriander seed. Put them with half a pound of loaf Sugar into a quart of Brandy. Add four ounces of stoned and bruised ripe black Cherries. Leave for three or four weeks, then strain and bottle.

CRAB APPLE WINE

Slice a gallon of Crab Apples with their skins

on and let them soak in a gallon of water for a fortnight. Then strain and to each gallon of the liquid add three pounds of Demerara Sugar. Stir well until fermentation takes place, which should be in a day or a day and a half. Leave for three days, and then put the wine into a cask or jar, putting a piece of muslin over the opening until the hissing noise made by the fermentation ceases. Then cork tightly, and bottle after three months.

DAMSON GIN

1 bottle London Gin
1 lb. Damsons
1 lb. Sugar

Prick the Damsons, and put them into a jar with the Sugar and Gin. Cork and seal tightly, and be sure to shake the jar gently each day for a fortnight. Then put by for a year, when the Gin may be strained and bottled.

DANDELION WINE

Gather the flowers on a fine day, and have a gallon of flowers to a gallon of water. Boil together for twenty minutes, then strain through muslin on to three pounds of Demerara Sugar. When the Sugar is dissolved, boil up again, and

see that the wine measures exactly one gallon.
Strain again into an earthenware jar, and add two
Oranges and two Lemons both sliced, and when
the wine is nearly cold add half an ounce of Yeast
on a bit of toast. Stand covered with a cloth for
three days, and stir well each day. Then strain
into bottles and cork tightly. The bottles should
be undisturbed for six months.

COWSLIP WINE

For every two gallons of water you must allow
two and a half pounds of Sugar and four quarts of
Cowslip flowers. Put the water and Sugar into a
pan, and boil for half an hour, skimming carefully. Then pour the liquor into a tub over the
thinly peeled rind of the Lemons and the Cowslip
flowers. Cover and leave for two days, stirring
well every two or three hours. Then pour into a
barrel and leave for a month. Put a lump of Sugar
in each bottle when you come to bottle the wine,
and be sure that you use only the tops of the
flowers.

CRANBERRY CORDIAL

Take a pint of Cranberry juice and add to it the
thinly peeled rind of an Orange, a bruised inch-

HOME-MADE DRINKS

stick of Cinnamon and half a dozen Cloves. Pour this into a jar with a quart of Whisky, cover closely and leave to infuse for a month. Then strain into bottles, and cork down tightly.

ELDERFLOWER CHAMPAGNE

A reader of mine sends me the following with the assurance that it is extremely good.

2 large heads of Elderflower, in full bloom
1 gallon cold Water
1 Lemon
2 tablespoonfuls White Vinegar
1½ lb. lump Sugar

Squeeze the juice from the Lemon, and cut the rind into four pieces. Put this with the flowers, Sugar, and Vinegar, into a large jar or pan, pour on the water and leave for twenty-four hours. Strain, and bottle in screw-stoppered bottles, and keep for several weeks before using.

GINGER BEER (I)

Bruise four dozen of whole Ginger, put it into two gallons of water and boil for two hours. Now add four pounds of lump Sugar and a quarter of a pound of Honey, let it boil for five minutes more and strain it through a cloth into a pan, earthenware being best. Add two and a half gallons of boiling water and the strained juice of a dozen Lemons. Let it stand, covered, for four days, then bottle it, wiring or tying the corks down. In a few days you can drink it. It is wiser to lay the bottles on their sides.

GINGER BEER (II)

Mix together one and three-quarter pounds of granulated Sugar, three teaspoonfuls of ground Ginger, and two teaspoonfuls of Cream of Tartar. Pour on a gallon of boiling water and stir until all is dissolved. Let it cool, then add half an ounce of yeast dissolved in half a teaspoonful of Castor Sugar. Cover and leave for twenty-four hours, skim if necessary, and pour gently off so as to leave the sediment behind. Bottle and cork, and in ordinary weather it will be ready to drink in a couple of days.

GINGER CORDIAL

Mash up a pound of picked White Currants, and put them into a bowl with an ounce and a half of ground Ginger, a pound of lump Sugar, and a quart of Brandy or Whisky. Leave for twenty-four hours or longer, then strain through a jelly-bag, and bottle. It improves by keeping.

HOME-MADE DRINKS

GOOSEBERRY WINE

'To every three pounds of Gooseberries a pound of Sugar and a quart of water. Bruise the Gooseberries and steep them twenty-four hours in the water. Then strain it out through a hair sieve into an earthen pot with a tap in it, and to the clear liquor so strained put your Sugar. Then cover the pot very close, and let it stand for a fortnight. Then draw it out into bottles, and put a little Sugar to it in the bottling: be sure you cork it well; you may drink it in a month, but it will keep good a year.'

GRAPE CORDIAL

To each quart of unfermented Grape juice allow a tablespoonful each of Cloves, Cinnamon, and Allspice. Boil up, cool and add (for each quart) half a pint of Brandy. Bottle and cork well.

GRAPE WINE

An old English recipe runs: When the vines are well grown, as to bring full clusters, be careful to take off some of those leaves which too much shade the grapes, but not in the hot seasons lest the sun should too swiftly draw away their juices and wither them. Stay not till they are ripe all at once, for then some will be over-ripe, and bruise or rot before the underlings come to perfection; but every two or three days pick off the ripest Grapes, and spread them in a shady place that they may not be burnt by the heat. Thus those that remain on the vine, having more heat to nourish them, will grow larger and be sooner ripe, and when you have got a sufficient quantity put them into an open vessel and bruise them well with your hands; or if the quantity be too great, get a flat piece of wood, fasten it to the end of a staff, and gently press them with it, taking care to break the stones as little as possible as that would give the wine a bitter taste. Having bruised the Grapes so that they become a pulp, you must have a tap at the bottom of your cask; then tie a hair-cloth over your receiving tub and let that out which will run off of itself, which will be found to be the best. Then take out the pulp, and press it by degrees till the liquor is sufficiently drained off, after which get a clean cask, well matched, and pour the liquor in through a sieve and funnel to stop the dregs, letting it stand with a slate over the bung-hole, to ferment and refine for ten or twelve days. Then draw it off gently into another cask, and put a slate over the bung-hole as before until the fermentation be over, which you may know by its coolness and pleasant taste. . . .

HOME-MADE DRINKS

GREEN GOOSEBERRY WINE

'Take thirty-two quarts of green Gooseberries, rinse them well, add thirty-two quarts of water, let them stand for twenty-four hours. Drain the Gooseberries well, through a sieve, put three and a half pounds of loaf Sugar to every gallon of liquor, and put it in a cask with a bottle of the best Gin. Let it stand for six months, and then bottle it. Mind to cork it well.'

That author's contention is that it is the equal of Champagne!

HAWTHORN BERRY WINE

Clean the berries, put them into an earthenware jar, pour over a pint of boiling water for each pound of the berries, and leave for six weeks. Now remove the crust, strain the liquid finely and add a pound of Sugar for each pound of the fruit originally used. Leave until fermentation stops, and then bottle, and keep as long as you can before using it.

HIGHLAND CORDIAL

Nathaniel Gubbins in his *Cakes and Ale* gives a cordial which is worth trying. 'Ingredients, one pint of White Currants, stripped of their stalks, the thin rind of a Lemon, one teaspoonful of Essence of Ginger, and one bottle of old Scotch Whisky. Let the mixture stand for forty-eight hours, and then strain through a hair sieve. Add one pound of loaf Sugar, which will take at least a day to thoroughly dissolve. Then bottle off and cork well. It will be ready for use in three months, but will keep longer.'

LEMON BRANDY

Allow the rinds of four Lemons to each pint of French Brandy. The rinds should be peeled off as thinly as possible, and then put into a bottle with the Brandy, tightly corked and left for a fortnight. Then strain off the spirit and re-bottle it.

LEMON GIN

Put the rinds of five Lemons, spread very thinly, into a jar with a pound of loaf Sugar and two and a half pints of Gin. Stir for ten minutes each day for twelve days, then strain and bottle. If you like, you can add the juice of all or some of the lemons.

MANGEL-WURZEL WINE

Wash and scrub absolutely clean ten pounds of

Mangel-Wurzels. Do not peel them, and cut them in slices. Add an ounce of dried Hops and two ounces of well-bruised root Ginger. Boil with enough water to cover the slices well for two hours, then strain through a jelly-bag, add enough water to make up a gallon, and stir in two pounds of brown Sugar until it is dissolved. Let cool, and put in an ounce of dried Yeast, leaving the wine to ferment in an open cask. When the fermentation stops, skim the wine well, add a bunch of dried Raisins, bung up well and keep for six months.

MULBERRY BRANDY

To each quart of Mulberry juice allow a quart of Brandy and a pound of Sugar. Let it stand for six weeks, then filter and bottle.

NECTAR

1 lb. juicy Raisins
2 lb. lump Sugar
1 gallon boiling Water
1 large Lemon

Cut the Raisins in four, put them into a pan with the Sugar, and pour the boiling water over them. Leave the pan covered with a cloth until the next day. Next morning add the Lemon thinly sliced. Stir as often as you can for the next five days, replacing the cloth each time, and then leave covered for another five days without stirring. Strain and bottle. Cork loosely for the first few days, then cork down tightly. It will be ready to drink in a few weeks' time.

NETTLE BEER

Pick plenty of young nettles, and boil them with enough water to cover them well, straining off the liquid from the pulp after a few minutes. Measure this, and to each quart add an ounce of ground Ginger, half an ounce of Cream of Tartar, the juice of a Lemon and half a pound of lump Sugar. Boil again for five minutes, then leave to cool and strain through a jelly-bag. Stir in a little Yeast, and leave the beer to ferment overnight. Then strain again, and bottle.

ORANGE BRANDY

'To a gallon of Brandy add two whole bitter Oranges. Leave them in the Brandy for six or even eight weeks. Then strain, taking out the fruit, and add one pound of Sugar Candy.'

HOME-MADE DRINKS

ORANGE GIN

Pare very thinly eight Seville Oranges and eight Lemons. Pour over these rinds a gallon of unsweetened Gin and add three pounds of loaf Sugar. Stir every day for a week, then strain and bottle.

ORANGE WINE

Wipe twenty-six Oranges and cut them in slices, taking out the pips. Put them into a tub, and pour two gallons of boiling water over them, then cover the tub and leave it for a week, stirring the contents frequently. Then strain through a jelly-bag, measure and add Sugar in the proportion of two pounds to each gallon of the liquor. Let it dissolve, pour the wine into a cask, and leave it until it stops fermenting. It will be ready to bottle in about four months' time.

PLUM WINE

Allow three pounds of ripe Plums to each gallon of water. Cut the Plums in half and pour boiling water over them. Leave them in the pan for four or five days or until they begin to ferment slightly. Then strain off the fruit and add three pounds of Sugar to each gallon of wine. When the sugar is dissolved, put the wine in a cask and let it ferment for a week or more. Then cork down and leave for six months or more.

QUINCE WINE

Grate twenty Quinces, leaving the core, and throw them into a gallon of boiling water. Simmer for twenty minutes, then pour the liquor into a jelly-bag, and press it through, squeezing the pulp well. Now pour this liquor over two pounds of preserving Sugar (the actual proportion is two pounds of Sugar to a gallon of the liquor), add the thinly peeled rind and the juice of two Lemons, and stir until nearly cold. Put in a little Yeast spread on a piece of toast, cover, and leave for twenty-four hours. Pour into a cask, taking out the rind and Yeast. Leave the cask open until fermentation stops, then close it up and keep as long as possible before bottling, as the wine improves with keeping.

RASPBERRY VINEGAR (LADY JEKYLL)

Take one pound of Raspberries for every pint of best White Wine Vinegar. Let it stand for a fortnight in a covered jar in a cool larder. Then strain without pressure, and to every pint put three-quarters of a pound of white Sugar. Boil ten minutes, let cool, and bottle.

This is 'specially suitable for the young after tennis or sports on a hot day, but acceptable also to the elders when exhausted by church, depressed by gardening, or exasperated by shopping'.

RATAFIA OF APRICOTS

Take twenty-five Apricots cut in pieces, break the stones and take out the kernels. Peel and crush these in a mortar and put them into a stoppered jar with the pieces of Apricot, half a pound of Sugar, eight Cloves, some Cinnamon, and a quart of Brandy. Put the stopper in closely, and leave it for three weeks, shaking the jar very often. Then strain and bottle.

RATAFIA OF PEACHES

Simply substitute Peaches for Apricots in the above recipe.

RHUBARB CHAMPAGNE

Bruise your Rhubarb stalks well, and to every nine pounds add a gallon of cold water. After steeping for a week in a covered pan, stirring twice a day, squeeze through a coarse cloth. To every gallon of liquor add four pounds of lump Sugar, put into a cask, and let it ferment for two or three weeks.

SHERRY TONIC

Strip some Hops from their stalks and fill some wide-necked bottles with them, up to the neck. Fill up with Sherry. Infuse for twenty-one days, then strain, and bottle.

SHRUB

½ gallon Rum
¾ pint Orange juice
½ pint Lemon juice
The peel of two Lemons
2 lb. loaf Sugar
2½ pints Water

Slice the Lemon peel very thinly, and put it with the fruit juice and Rum into a large covered jar. Let it stand for two days, then pour over it the water in which you have dissolved the Sugar, remove the Lemon peel, and leave for a fortnight before using.

SLOE GIN

Wash well and prick all over three quarts of Sloes, and put them into a jar with two and a half pounds of Sugar, half an ounce of bitter Almonds and a gallon of unsweetened Gin. Shake frequently, and finally bottle. Keep it as long as you can before drinking.

STRAWBERRY LIQUEUR

Have ready some wide-necked bottles and half fill them with ripe perfect Strawberries previously pricked with a darning-needle. Add an equal amount of Sugar Candy and fill the bottles with Brandy. Cork tightly and let stand in a warm place for six weeks. Then strain, and bottle.

TOMATO WINE

Cut fresh ripe Tomatoes in pieces with a silver or stainless steel knife, mash well, and leave to drain on a sieve. When the liquid has all run through, add a little Salt and some cane Sugar to taste. Stir now and then until the Sugar has dissolved, then pour into a jar just large enough to hold it, and cover, leaving a small opening for the fermentation to work through. When this has ceased the liquor should be pure and clear. Pour into bottles, cork tightly and set aside for a while before drinking.

HOME-MADE DRINKS

WHORTLEBERRY WINE

Allow a gallon of water for each gallon of berries, and two pounds of Sugar to each gallon of juice. Pour the boiling water over the berries, cover them and leave them all night. Then strain and press out the juice, measure it, add the Sugar, let it dissolve, and pour the liquor into a cask. Cover the bung-hole lightly, and when fermentation has ceased, bung up and leave for nine months. The wine should be filtered on bottling.

VEGETABLE WINES

VEGETABLE WINES

BEETROOT WINE

Wash four pounds of Beetroots, cut them in pieces, and put them into cold water, allowing a quart for every pound. Boil until the colour is extracted and then strain the liquor off. Now to every quart of it, add half a pound of lump Sugar, the juice of a Lemon, four or five Cloves, and a root of Ginger. Stir until the Sugar is dissolved, spread half an ounce of Yeast on toast, put in when lukewarm and keep covered for a fortnight, stirring each day. Skim well, then bottle and cover lightly until fermentation stops. Then cork down and keep for twelve months before drinking.

CARROT WINE

Here is 'A Lady's' (1886) recipe for 18 gallons of Carrot Wine, proof at any rate that it was popular! The ingredients may of course be decreased, proportionately.

VEGETABLE WINES

'Take one hundred and twenty pounds of Carrots, wash and slice them, then boil them in twenty-three gallons of water for two hours, then strain the liquor from them, add to it half a hundred of brown Sugar, boil it again for fifteen minutes, and put to it six Eggs to break it, when cool put to it one quart of fresh Yeast, work it ten days, stirring it once a day, then put it in the cask, and bottle it in twelve months.'

PARSLEY WINE

For every pound of Parsley, add a gallon of boiling water, let this stand for twenty-four hours, and then strain off the liquor. Boil this for twenty minutes with an ounce of root Ginger, the rind of two Oranges and two Lemons. Let it get nearly cool, and then put in half an ounce of Yeast on a piece of toast, and let it stand for four days. Then strain it, bottle it and finally cork down only when the Wine has stopped working. It is all the better for keeping.

PARSNIP WINE

Make this of young Parsnips in the spring, clean and peel them, rinse them in cold water and cut them in thin slices. Boil them in an open pan until they are quite tender, allowing a gallon of water to each five pounds of the slices, then strain off the liquor, pressing out all the liquid and straining it again through a jelly-bag. Put the liquid into a preserving-pan with three pounds of preserving Sugar to each gallon of it, and boil again for three-quarters of an hour. Pour this into your pan or tub, and when lukewarm put in a slice of toast spread with half an ounce or so of Yeast. Cover with a thick cloth or blanket, and leave for ten days, stirring each day. Then strain into a cask, and keep filling up until fermentation has stopped. Then close tightly, and leave for at least six months before bottling. Parsnip Wine is said to taste like Sherry. It may look like a pale Sherry, but I doubt if it would ever deceive any one—who had ever tasted Sherry. Such comparisons are all wrong. If we like Parsnip Wine, we drink it as Parsnip Wine. Our favourities should need no excuses.

PEA-POD WINE

The peculiar wine was found for me, where I know not, by a friend who heard I was contemplating this book.

Put a gallon of pea-pods in a gallon of cold water, with a sliced Lemon and half a dozen Cloves. Boil until the pods are tender, then strain and to every gallon of the liquid add four pounds of lump Sugar. When cool, add a teaspoonful of Yeast on a piece of toast, leave for twenty-four hours, and then bottle. Leave for a long time before drinking.

POTATO WINE

Take a gallon of warm water, and put into it two large and finely grated potatoes, four pounds of Demerara Sugar, two pounds of Raisins, a pint of clean new Wheat, the juice and grated rind of two Lemons, and an ounce of Yeast. Leave this to stand for three weeks, stirring it now and then. Then strain it through a jelly-bag, and bottle. In about a month's time, the wine will clear, then add a little Sugar Candy to each bottle. It may then soon be used, but will be all the better for keeping.

RHUBARB BRANDY

Peel six pounds of Rhubarb, cut it in small pieces and weigh it. Cover it with a gallon of water, and add half a pound of chopped Raisins. Leave for a fortnight, stirring and mashing the Rhubarb each day, then squeeze the liquor from the Rhubarb, and leave it, with the Raisins, half a dozen broken Egg-shells and four pounds of lump Sugar for another week. Then skim, and bottle, and in four months it will be ready.

VEGETABLE WINES

RHUBARB WINE

Cut five pounds of Rhubarb into short pieces, and bruise and chop them, putting them into a bowl with a gallon of cold water. Leave for five days, stirring now and then. Then strain the liquor, and dissolve in it by stirring three pounds of lump Sugar. Add the yellow part of the rind of two Lemons and an ounce of Isinglass. Leave for five days, skim, pour into a cask and leave unstopped for about a fortnight. Then close, and you can begin to use the wine in about six months. The colour may be deepened if liked with Currant juice.

SWEDE WINE

Here is a wine I am told may be made from Swedes or Mangel-Wurzels. Wash well and scrub quite clean enough Swedes to make ten pounds when cut unpeeled in slices. Boil these in enough water to cover them well, adding an ounce of dried Hops and two ounces of well-bruised root Ginger, for two hours. Then strain through a jelly-bag, add sufficient water to make up to a gallon, add then two pounds of brown Sugar, and stir it until it is dissolved. When cool, add an ounce of dried Yeast, and let the wine ferment in an open cask. When fermentation is over, skim it well, add a bunch of dried Raisins, stop closely, and keep for six months before using.

TOMATO WINE

Remove the stalks from some fresh ripe Tomatoes, cut them in pieces with a stainless steel knife, mash them up well, and put them in a sieve to drain. When all the juice has run out, add a little Salt, and cane Sugar to taste. Let the Sugar dissolve, stirring now and then, then put the juice into a porcelain jar or jug, filling it nearly full. Cover closely, leaving a small opening for the scum to rise from when fermentation begins. Leave until fermentation stops, and the liquid is clear. Pour into bottles, cork tightly, and leave for some time before using.

TURNIP WINE

Peel and slice the Turnips thinly. Sprinkle the slices with a little Sugar, and leave them all night. Press out all the juice, measure it, and add three pounds of cane preserving Sugar for every gallon of Turnip juice. Add half a pint of Brandy for this quantity, pour the mixture into a clean, dry cask just large enough to hold it, cover lightly until it has stopped working, then stop, and leave for three months before bottling. A year should elapse before you drink it.

CURIOUS DRINKS

CURIOUS DRINKS

BRAZIL RELISH

Into a wineglassful of Curaçao drop the un-broken yolk of a bantam's egg. Fill up the glass with Maraschino.

(Morituri, te salutamus!)

BUNNY HUG COCKTAIL

⅓ Gin
⅓ Whisky
⅓ Absinthe

COCKTAIL (Francatelli)

'Put three lumps of Sugar into a tumbler with a dessertspoonful of Savory and Moore's Essence of Jamaica Ginger, and a wineglassful of Brandy; fill up with hot water.'

CURE FOR DRUNKENNESS

5 grains Sulphate of Iron

CURIOUS DRINKS

16 grains Magnesia
11 drachma Peppermint Water
1 drachm Spirit of Nutmeg
  Dose: a wineglassful twice a day.

DRINK FOR THE FIDGETS (1808)

2 drachms Camphor
1 teaspoonful Spirits of Wine.

Put a pint of boiling water to it, and take a coffee-cup of it twice a day.

FARMER'S JOY

Put a pint of Sherry into a large bowl, dissolve in it two ounces of Sugar and flavour it with a little grated Nutmeg. Milk the cow into the bowl until you have added about two quarts of milk, then stir it up well and drink it.

HOCK CUP

3 bottles of Hock
1 Sherry-glassful Liqueur Brandy
1 dessertspoonful Crème de Menthe
1 tablespoonful Gin
3 peeled, stoned, and sliced Peaches
A few Strawberries
  Ice well. Decorate with a few sprigs of Borage.

CURIOUS DRINKS

KING WILLIAM'S POSSET

Beat the yolks of ten Eggs and the whites of four, and add them to a quart of Cream and a pint of Ale. Sweeten to taste, and grate some Nutmeg into the mixture. Bring nearly to the boil, stirring all the time, and when it is thick serve it from a bowl.

KITTY HIGHBALL

Claret and Ginger Ale
(This is Prohibition getting its own back!)

MOUNTAIN OYSTER

Mix together:

2 teaspoons Worcester Sauce
2 teaspoons Brandy
1 teaspoon Vinegar
1 teaspoon Tomato Ketchup

Add yolk of fresh Egg without breaking it, and dust a little Cayenne Pepper on top.

PICK-ME-UP

Put one or two pieces of ice in a tumbler, add the juice of a Lemon, the same quantity of Worcester Sauce, and fill up with Soda Water.

CURIOUS DRINKS

PRIMA DONNA

Beat the yolk of an Egg in a glass of Sherry, and serve with a dash of Cayenne Pepper.

SCORCHER

Juice of half a Lemon
1 liqueur-glassful old Brandy
Serve with a dash of Cayenne Pepper.

SPLIT WORCESTER

A small wineglassful of Worcester Sauce with a split Soda.

TEXAS HIGHBALL

$\frac{1}{2}$ bourbon Whisky
$\frac{1}{2}$ Port
Serve with a little ice (!!!)

THUNDERCLAP COCKTAIL

2 glasses Brandy
2 glasses Gin
2 glasses Whisky
Shake well and serve.

CURIOUS DRINKS

TIGER'S MILK (I)

A wineglassful of Peach Brandy and half a wineglassful each of Cider and Irish Whisky are mixed in a tumbler, and there is added to them an Egg white which has been beaten up with a little Sugar. The tumbler is then filled up with ice, shaken and the contents strained. To them is finally added half a tumblerful of Milk, and a little Nutmeg is grated over the top.

TIGER'S MILK (II)

I am indebted to Lady Sysonby's Cook Book for this peculiar drink. Beat up the yolks of three Eggs with half a pint of Brandy, a wineglass of powdered Sugar, a bit of thin Lemon peel, a dozen cloves and Cardamoms. Add a quart of new Milk, grate in a third of a Nutmeg, and serve in a tankard, of which see the bottom before removing from the lips!

WAIT A BIT

1 pint bottle of Scotch Ale
1 bottle aerated Lemonade
1 pint of ice in lumps

A NOTE ON WINE

A NOTE ON WINE

THE art of drinking Wine and understanding it implies a range of knowledge and experience which unfits it for inclusion in this volume. To attempt to deal with the subject in the briefest manner would be as unsatisfactory to the reader as it would be difficult—almost impossible—for the writer.

It has been thought best, therefore, to refer those readers who are interested in or seek knowledge of the subject to the list of books dealing with it, which appears at the end of this anthology. There they will find all the information they desire set out at a length which this book could never attempt. The list in question is given on pages 227-230.

PART II
SOFT DRINKS

COCKTAILS

COCKTAILS

CHOIRBOY

The juice of half an Orange
The juice of quarter of a Lemon
Grenadine to taste
Possibly a touch of Sugar
  Ice and shake.

CLAM JUICE COCKTAIL

Add to an eight-ounce bottle of Clam Bouillon
a tablespoonful of Tomato Ketchup, a pinch of
Celery Salt, and a dash of Tabasco Sauce. Ice and
shake.

FRUIT JUICE COCKTAIL

6 tablespoonfuls Grapefruit juice
4 tablespoonfuls Orange juice
$\frac{1}{2}$ pint Water
2 tablespoonfuls Sugar

COCKTAILS

A pinch of Salt
A few sprigs of Mint

Mix juice, Sugar, and Salt together. Bruise the Mint, add it to the water for a few minutes, then take it out and mix the water with the juice. Chill well and serve with a Mint leaf in each cocktail glass.

GINGER COCKTAIL

5 tablespoonfuls Ginger syrup
2 tablespoonfuls Orange juice
1½ tablespoonfuls Lemon juice
1 gill Soda Water

Shake together, and pour into cocktail glasses over crushed ice.

LEMON COCKTAIL

5 glasses sweetened Lemon juice
1 teaspoonful Angostura Bitters

LIME JUICE COCKTAIL

2½ tablespoonfuls Lime juice
1½ gills Ginger Ale
2 tablespoonfuls Orange juice
2 tablespoonfuls Sugar syrup

Shake and pour out into crushed ice.

COCKTAILS

ORANGE COCKTAIL

4 glasses Orange juice
A pinch of Mixed Spice
A few drops of Orange Bitters
Put a Maraschino Cherry in each glass

PARSON'S SPECIAL

1 glass Orange juice
4 dashes Grenadine
1 Egg yolk

PRAIRIE HEN

Put in a glass in this order:
2 dashes Vinegar
1 teaspoonful Worcester Sauce
1 whole unbroken Egg
2 dashes Tabasco Sauce
Salt and Pepper

SAUERKRAUT JUICE COCKTAIL

Add Lemon juice to taste to Sauerkraut juice.
Serve very cold.

THREE FRUIT COCKTAIL

5 tablespoonfuls Grapefruit juice
2 tablespoonfuls Orange juice

COCKTAILS

1 tablespoonful Lemon juice
3 tablespoonfuls Sugar syrup
A few grains of Salt
A gill of Soda Water
Shake well together, and pour out in glasses over crushed ice. Garnish with a sprig of Mint.

TOMATO COCKTAIL (I)

3 breakfastcupfuls of Tomato *purée*
2 sticks of Celery
1 tablespoonful chopped Onion
1 tablespoonful chopped Green Pepper (Pimento)
1 teaspoonful of Sugar
$\frac{1}{8}$ teaspoonful of Salt
$\frac{1}{4}$ teaspoonful of Pepper
Simmer together in a covered saucepan for a quarter of an hour. Strain and chill well before serving.

TOMATO COCKTAIL (II)

1 breakfastcupful fresh Tomato juice
1 tablespoonful mild Vinegar
1 tablespoonful Lemon juice
2 teaspoonfuls of Sugar

COCKTAILS

1 teaspoonful minced Onion
1 bruised Celery stick
A tiny bit of Bayleaf
   Mix together, stand for a quarter of an hour, and strain. Chill and serve.

TOMATO COCKTAIL (III)

Tomato juice
Dash of Yorkshire Relish
Suspicion of Cayenne Pepper
Spot of Chilli Vinegar

COLD DRINKS

COLD DRINKS

A FRUIT DRINK (I)

For this you want a cupful each of Strawberries or Raspberries, Red or White Currants, and stoned Cherries. Mash the fruit to a pulp, and add the strained juice of a Lemon and a teacupful of Castor Sugar. Boil up two quarts of water, pour it over the fruit and let it stand for at least four hours. Then strain and chill.

A FRUIT DRINK (II)

'Have you ever tasted', asks a writer in one of our weeklies, 'a summer drink made from the juice left over from any stewed fruit (particularly Plums), with Lemon and Orange juice added to taste, and the glass filled up with Soda? Two or three tablespoonfuls in an ordinary tumbler is the right quantity.'

Not if I can help it. But it might be an idea worth considering in a grave emergency.

169

COLD DRINKS

ALMOND WATER

Put six ounces of ground Sweet Almonds in a pan with two ounces of Bitter Almonds and one quart of water. Simmer for a quarter of an hour. Add one pound loaf Sugar, broken small, and when dissolved, strain. When cold it is ready. A tablespoonful of Orange-flower water is a great improvement. Proportions: half a teacupful in a tumbler filled up with Soda Water.

A LONG FRUIT DRINK

Take a pint tumbler, and put into it a tablespoonful of Strawberry juice. Add a tablespoonful of Cream or Milk, and fill up with Soda Water.

You can use Oranges or Pineapple or any other fruit in this way, if you prefer.

APPLE TREE DULCET

Put two or three tablespoonfuls of Apple juice, sweetened to your taste, into a tumbler with a few pieces of ice, and fill up with Ginger Ale or Cider. If you like, top this drink with the stiffly whisked white of an Egg, and garnish with a tiny sprig of Mint.

COLD DRINKS

BLACKBERRY DRINK

Put into a large tumbler a quarter of a wine-glassful of Blackberry juice, a teaspoonful of Lemon juice and a tablespoonful or more of fine Sugar. Fill up to two-thirds with shaved ice. Shake well and fill up with Iced or Soda Water.

CANTON LEMONADE

Boil together a breakfastcup and a half of Sugar, half a teaspoonful of ground Ginger and a pint of water until they make a syrup, and then add half a cupful of Lemon juice. Let this get cool, and use at once or bottle. A couple of tablespoonfuls to an ordinary glass of water should be enough.

CHERRY DRINK (I)

Pound up a pound of Cherries in a mortar, and put them into a large jug with four ounces of Castor Sugar and a small stick of Cinnamon. Pour over them a quart of boiling water, and strain when cold. Serve iced.

CHERRY DRINK (II)

Stone and mash a pound of Cherries, and add

to them four dessertspoonfuls of Honey, the juice of a Lemon and six breakfastcupfuls of boiling water. Cool, strain, and serve very cold.

EAU DE FRAISES

See page 50.

FIGS AND APPLES

Split in half six dried Figs and put them into a pan with a sliced unpeeled Apple and half a pound of lump Sugar. Add two quarts of water, bring to the boil and boil for two minutes. Strain it, and keep it covered until cold.

GINGER ALE AND ANGOSTURA

Well-iced Dry Ginger Ale with a spot or so of Angostura Bitters makes a good summer drink.

GRAPE JUICE

If you don't want to buy a proprietary brand of Grape juice, such as Welch's, you can make it like this: Put ten pounds of Grapes and a breakfastcupful of water into a thick stewpan, heat until the stones and pulp separate; then strain through a

COLD DRINKS

jelly-bag, add three pounds of Sugar, heat to boiling point, and bottle. This will make a gallon. Dilute fifty-fifty with water when serving.

GRAPE JUICE AND GINGER ALE

Half Ginger Ale and half Grape juice (homemade or Welch's) makes an excellent drink, says Margery Wren.

GRENADINE FRAPPE

Mix four tablespoonfuls of Grenadine with a teaspoonful of Lemon juice. Fill a tall glass three-quarters full of shaved ice, pour over the Grenadine and Lemon, and serve.

HORSE'S NECK (DISPIRITED!)

Put the peel of a Lemon in a tumbler with one end hanging over the top of the glass, add two lumps of broken ice, and fill up with cold Ginger Ale.

ICED CHOCOLATE

Make your Chocolate according to any good

COLD DRINKS

recipe, let it get cold, and pour it over some crushed ice. Stir well and sweeten to taste. Serve, if you like, with whipped cream.

ICED TEA

Make some Indian Tea in the usual manner, but only let the leaves infuse for just under one minute. Pour off the tea on to some Lemon peel and Sugar (as if you were making Lemonade), and when it is cold put it into a jug with plenty of broken ice, and serve it with a sprig or two of Mint floating on top.

JAM FRUIT DRINKS

An impromptu drink can be made with jams . . . but they are only recommended in an emergency! Strain them after mixing and then chill them.

Raspberry: 1 quart warm water, two tablespoonfuls Raspberry jam or jelly, the juice of four Lemons and Sugar to taste.

Red Currant: As above, but no Lemon juice.

Black Currant: As above, no Lemon juice.

Red Gooseberry: As above, but only one Lemon.

Blackberry: As above, only one Lemon.

COLD DRINKS

LEMONADE

Pare two Lemons very thinly and put the rind with an ounce of Sugar into a jug. Pour on it a pint of boiling water, let it remain covered until it is cold, then add the juice of the Lemons. Strain before serving.

(If you leave this in the jug long enough, it will cease to be non-alcoholic, and will become rather pleasant.)

LEMONADE (American)

Put in a tumbler the strained juice of one Lemon, a tablespoonful and a half of Icing Sugar and a wineglass of cold water. Fill up three parts with shaved ice, and shake well. Then fill up with Soda Water, adding a dash of Strawberry syrup and decorating with a thin slice of Lemon.

MINT COOLER

1 pint Ginger Ale
1 bunch lightly bruised Mint
1 lump ice

MULBERRY DRINK

Mash a pint of Mulberries in the juice of two

COLD DRINKS

Lemons, add a pint of water and a little syrup. Strain through a hair sieve.

Strawberries and Raspberries may be used in the same way.

MULE'S COLLAR

Juice of a Lime
Dash of Angostura Bitters
3 lumps of ice
1 bottle Dry Ginger Ale

ORANGEADE (I)

Put the rind of two thinly peeled Oranges into a saucepan with a gill of water and a couple of ounces of Sugar. Boil together for a little while to get the flavour into the water, then strain into a jug, adding the juice of four Oranges, a pint and three-quarters of cold water and, when it is quite cold, half a siphon of Soda Water.

ORANGEADE (II)

Squeeze the juice from four Oranges and one Lemon, and strain it into a jug with half a pound of Sugar. Pour in a quart of boiling water, and stir until the Sugar dissolves.

COLD DRINKS

ORANGE AND HONEY

Slightly melt a tablespoonful of Honey, and stir it well and briskly with a third of a breakfast-cupful of Orange juice, a tablespoonful of Lemon juice, a small pinch of Salt, and a little crushed ice. Pour this quickly back and forth into a second jug, to get it well mixed and serve it in glasses with cracked ice and a garnish of shredded Orange rind.

PERSIAN SHERBET

Mash up a pound of Strawberries, wild ones being the best, and add slices of Lemon without the pips, a teaspoonful of Orange-flower water and finally half a pint of water. Cover and leave for three hours. Then strain through a cloth, pressing well, stir in half a pound of Sugar and go on stirring until it is all dissolved. Strain again, and keep on ice until wanted.

PINEAPPLE FIZZ

Pour a pint of boiling water over three-quarters of a pound of lump Sugar in a saucepan, and boil it for ten minutes. Mix the juice of two Lemons with a tin of crushed Pineapple and add this to the syrup. Put on the lid and leave until it is cold, then strain through muslin, and just before serving add three bottles of Soda Water and some chipped ice.

PRUNE WATER

. 4 oz. Prunes
½ small Lemon
Sugar
3 breakfastcupfuls Water

Slit each Prune down the side and put them into a pan with the thinly pared Lemon rind. Boil very slowly for half an hour, then add the juice of the Lemon-half, strain, sweeten to taste and let it get cold.

RHUBARB FLIP

Stir one cup of sweetened Rhubarb juice, one tablespoonful of Sugar and a dash of Nutmeg into three well-beaten Egg yolks, and pour over cracked ice into six tall glasses. Fill up with Ginger Ale and serve at once.

SARSAPARILLA COOLER

1 pint Sarsaparilla
Juice of half a Lime
3 or 4 round slices of Lime
1 large piece of ice

COLD DRINKS

SARSAPARILLA DRINK

Boil a quarter of a pound of Sarsaparilla Root,
well bruised, with two quarts of water until reduced to a quart. Then strain, and bottle when
cold. A tablespoonful to a glass of Soda Water is
the correct proportion.

STRAWBERRY DRINK

Strain into a tumbler the juice of a Lemon or an
Orange, add a dessertspoonful of Castor Sugar,
and a tablespoonful of Strawberry syrup. Finish
with shaved ice and Soda Water.

HOT DRINKS

HOT DRINKS

CHOCOLATE (SWEDISH METHOD)

Break a good two ounces of Chocolate into a saucepan, add a good pint each of Milk and Water and bring to the boil. Mix four level tablespoonfuls of Cocoa with three-quarters of a level tablespoonful of Potato Flour in a little cold water, and add this to the boiling Chocolate mixture, whisking well. When well boiling, add Sugar to taste. Serve hot, with a dollop of stiffly whisked vanilla-flavoured Cream on top.

COCOA-NIBS

Take two quarts of cold water to a teacupful of unbruised Cocoa-nibs, and let it simmer without boiling in an open saucepan until reduced by half. Add a pint of cold water and boil to reduce to half the quantity; then add a second pint of cold water, again reduce to half, and finally add a third pint, also reducing this to half. The lid must not be put on during this process, which will take five or six hours. The liquid should then be strained, and will be found to be a beautiful Claret colour. Serve with hot Milk, Cream, and Sugar.

LAIT DE POULE

Beat up an Egg yolk in a bowl with one or two teaspoonfuls of fine Castor Sugar. When the mixture looks like a thick white cream, add boiling water, whipping all the time. Flavour with Orangeflower water, or with Rum, and serve at once.

LEMONADE, HOT SPICED

Mix together the strained juice of half a Lemon, three teaspoonfuls of white Sugar, half a teaspoonful of ground Ginger, and one and a quarter breakfastcupfuls of boiling water. Stir up and serve.

MEXICAN CHOCOLATE

Mix two breakfastcupfuls of ordinary breakfast Cocoa with the same amount of black Coffee; add half a teaspoonful of Vanilla Essence, and serve with Whipped Cream.

HOT DRINKS

RAISIN TEA

Chop up coarsely half a pound of Raisins, and simmer them in a quart of water with the rind of a Lemon, slowly, until the liquid is reduced to a pint. Strain, add the juice of the Lemon, and serve either hot or cold.

CUPS

CUPS

APPLE CUP

Wash two pounds of Apples, and cut them up without first paring them. Put them into a pan with an ounce of Cinnamon Stick, the rind of one Lemon and the juice of two. Boil until soft, then mash up and strain off the liquid through a sieve. Dissolve four ounces of Sugar in every quart of liquid, and boil for a few minutes. Serve iced.

FRUIT CUP

Boil together half a pint of Pineapple juice with a quarter of a pound of Sugar for ten minutes. Cut up in small pieces:

1 Grapefruit
1 Apple
1 Orange
1 Banana
$\frac{1}{4}$ lb. Pineapple
$\frac{1}{4}$ lb. Grapes

Pour over the hot juice, add the juice of two Lemons and leave standing for twelve hours. Use in the proportion of one part of fruit juice to three parts of iced water or Soda Water, adding the cut-up fruit as well. Serve very cold.

GINGER ALE CUP

Put two bruised sprigs of Mint into a jug with crushed ice, moisten with a pint of Ginger Ale and the juice of half a Lemon, and decorate with thin slices from the Lemon's other half.

GRAPEFRUIT AND ORANGE CUP

Grate the rind off two Oranges with some lump Sugar, and put it into a jug with enough Sugar to make half a pound in all, the juice of the two scraped Oranges and of two more and the juice of two Grapefruit. Pour over a pint of boiling water, cover and leave until cold. Now add a pint of cold water, and strain the cup into another jug, in which you have put a lump of ice. Then just as you want it, throw in two sprigs of Mint and add a couple of bottles of Dry Ginger Ale.

PUSSYFOOT CUP

1 wineglassful of Orange juice

CUPS

1 wineglassful of Lemon juice
1 bottle Lemonade
2 bottles Soda Water
½ bottle Tonic Water
½ bottle Ginger Ale
  Decorate as any wine cup.

PUNCHES

PUNCHES

CARDINAL PUNCH

Cook a quart of Cranberries in four breakfast-cupfuls of water until they are soft, then mash them and drain them through a cheesecloth. Boil two breakfastcupfuls of Sugar with the same amount of water for five minutes, add this to the Cranberry juice and let it get cold. Now add a tablespoonful and a half of Lemon juice and a breakfastcupful of Orange juice. Just before serving very cold, pour in a quart of iced Ginger Ale.

CHOCOLATE PUNCH

½ breakfastcupful of Chocolate Extract
1 teaspoonful Sugar
1 Egg
Enough Milk to fill up the glass

Shake all together with ice, and strain into a glass.

ELDERBERRY PUNCH

2 bottles Elderberry Wine

PUNCHES

4 pounds Icing Sugar
3 pints boiling water
 After mixing well, add a thinly sliced Lemon
and a grating of Nutmeg.

GERMAN PUNCH (American style)

 Mix together a breakfastcupful each of Cider
and Grape juice and half a cupful of Grapefruit
juice. Add a quart of Soda Water, sweeten to taste
and pour into a bowl over a large piece of ice.

ICED TEA PUNCH

 Mix together:
1 pint China Tea
1 gill Claret
The juice of half a Lemon
3 slices of unpeeled Cucumber
Sugar to taste
 And stand on ice until wanted.

ORANGE PUNCH

 Put a good-sized piece of ice into a bowl, and
add a cupful of Orange juice and half a cupful of
Lemon juice (both strained) and as much Sugar
syrup as will sweeten it to your liking. Before

serving, add a pint of Ginger Ale and a pint of Soda Water and decorate with a few thin slices of Orange.

RED CURRANT PUNCH

Make a syrup with a pint of water and a pound of Sugar, add the juice of an Orange and a Lemon, strain and mix in half a pint of Red Currant juice, or a glass of Red Currant jelly. When it is cold, add shaved ice and Soda Water.

MINTFRUIT PUNCH

Loosely fill a pint pudding basin with fresh Mint leaves, wash and bruise them, put them into a jug with a quart of boiling water, stir and leave to stand for a quarter of an hour. Now strain this infusion, and add the juice of an Orange and a tea-cupful of any seasonable fruit juice, Strawberries, Raspberries, Red Currants, and add a little Castor Sugar until it is sweet enough. Serve very cold indeed, decorated with a few sprigs of Mint.

MULBERRY PUNCH

See *Elderberry Punch* (page 195), substituting Mulberry for Elderberry Wine.

PUNCHES

POMEGRANATE PUNCH

Squeeze the juice from four Lemons and two Oranges and dissolve in it a breakfastcupful of Sugar. Now add a quart of water, and put the mixture on ice until wanted. Then put a good lump of ice in a bowl and pour the liquid over it, stirring in a teacupful of Grenadine and a quart of Soda Water. Decorate with Strawberries.

TEA PUNCH

Add to a cup of strong tea a cup of sweetened Strawberry juice, half a cup of Orange juice and three tablespoonfuls of Lemon juice. Chill, and just before serving add a cup of iced Ginger Ale. Garnish the glasses with whole Strawberries.

COLD MILK DRINKS

The popularity of the Milk Bar in the past few years has given a new significance to milk drinks of various kinds. In this section there are given a small number of recipes which will enable the lover of milk to indulge his (or her) passion in various forms.

The recipes marked with an asterisk (*) are included by kind permission of the Milk Marketing Board.

COLD MILK DRINKS

MILK SHAKE

Put equal quantities of Milk and ice into a shaker, the Milk being flavoured with Vanilla and slightly sweetened. Add a dash of Soda Water, shake well, and decorate the glass with Whipped Cream and Strawberries or *glacé* Cherries.

* APPLE BLOSSOM

7 oz. Milk
One-fortieth quart Ice Cream (1 oz.)
2 tablespoonfuls of sieved stewed Apple
½ oz. Black Currant syrup
Dash of Soda Water
Add the Soda Water after the rest are mixed.

* BANANA CREAM WHIP

7 oz. Milk
One-fortieth quart Ice Cream (1 oz.)

COLD MILK DRINKS

Quarter of a Banana thinly sliced
1 teaspoonful Whipped Cream
1 *glacé* Cherry

Mix together first three, and decorate with the Cream and Cherry.

CHOCOLATE MILK SHAKE

Grate up two tablespoonfuls of the best Chocolate and mix to a paste with a little warm Milk, until quite smooth. Put a quarter of a cupful of finely chopped ice into a shaker, add half a cupful of Milk, a tablespoonful of Cream, the melted Chocolate with a little Castor Sugar added, and a dash of Soda Water. Shake together for five minutes and serve with a cap of Whipped Cream flavoured with Vanilla.

* CHOCOLATE MILK SHAKE

7 oz. Milk
¾ oz. liquid Chocolate
One-fortieth quart Ice Cream (1 oz.)
¼ oz. Vanilla

* COFFEE MILK SHAKE

7 oz. Milk

COLD MILK DRINKS

¾ oz. Coffee
¼ oz. Vanilla
One-fortieth quart Ice Cream (1 oz.)

* CREAM SNOWBALL

5 oz. Milk
One-fortieth quart Ice Cream (1 oz.)
½ oz. Crème de Menthe syrup
1 oz. Whipped Cream
  Mix all but half the Cream together, reserving this for garnishing.

* FRUIT SALAD SHAKE

7 oz. Milk
One-fortieth quart Ice Cream (1 oz.)
2 teaspoonfuls chopped tinned Fruit Salad

* GINGER FRAPPE

1 Egg
5 oz. Milk
½ oz. Lemon syrup
½ oz. Ginger syrup
1 teaspoonful Whipped Cream
  Mix together all but Cream, and decorate with this after.

COLD MILK DRINKS

* LOGANBERRY DELIGHT

7 oz. Milk
½ oz. Loganberry syrup
Dash of Orange syrup
Few slices of Cucumber
1 dessertspoonful crushed Loganberries

* PINEAPPLE MILK FRAPPE

6 oz. Milk
One-fortieth quart Ice Cream (1 oz.)
½ oz. Pineapple syrup.
2 teaspoonfuls crushed Pineapple
1 teaspoonful Whipped Cream
    Mix all but Cream, and decorate with this.

HOT MILK DRINKS

HOT MILK DRINKS

* APRICOT FLUFF

6 oz. hot Milk
¾ oz. Apricot syrup
1 Egg
   Whisk together Milk, syrup, and yolk of Egg.
Beat up the white separately, and pile on top of
the glass.

* AUTUMN GLORY

7 oz. hot Milk
½ oz. Chocolate syrup
1 tablespoonful chopped Pineapple
1 tablespoonful green-tinted nuts (chopped)
   Mix first three, and decorate with the nuts.

* CARAMEL CREAM WHIP

7 oz. hot Milk
¾ oz. Caramel syrup

2 tablespoonfuls Whipped Cream

Mix first two with half the Cream, and serve with the rest of the Cream as garnish.

* EGG MARASCHINO

¾ oz. Maraschino syrup
1 Egg
7 oz. hot Milk
1 teaspoonful grated Nutmeg

Whip syrup, Egg and hot Milk together, and serve with the grated Nutmeg on top.

* EGYPTIAN FLIP

1 teaspoonful Honey
1 teaspoonful ground Almonds
½ teaspoonful powdered Cinnamon
7 oz. hot Milk
1 teaspoonful Whipped Cream

Mix all ingredients except the Cream together, and serve with the Whipped Cream on top.

* MILK AMBROSIA

7 oz. hot Milk
¾ oz. Ginger syrup

HOT MILK DRINKS

1 teaspoonful Honey
1 tablespoonful Cream
  Whisk all together.

* SAVOURY SHAKE

1 tablespoonful Tomato Sauce
1 teaspoonful Worcestershire Sauce
Pinch of Salt
7 oz. hot Milk

This shake was the second-prize winner in the *Daily Mail* National Milk Shake Competition, 1935.

FRUIT MILK DRINKS

The following recipes are taken, by kind permission of the National Milk Publicity Council, from their booklet 'Milk Recipes'

These drinks can be made with the juice of fresh or stewed fruits and cold or hot (not boiling) Milk. Put the Milk into a bowl, and add the fruit juice a drop at a time, beating briskly. The proportions are an ounce to an ounce and a half of fruit juice to half a pint of Milk. For this quantity a teaspoonful of Ice Cream may be added to the cold drinks.

FRUIT MILK DRINKS

FRUIT MILK DRINK (with essence)

½ pint Milk
½ oz. Pineapple Essence
2 tablespoonfuls Ice Cream
Combine ingredients and beat with an Egg-whisk. Serve with grated Nutmeg on top.
  Alternative flavourings suggested are:

Raspberry	Cherry
Banana	Orange
Lemon	Crème de Menthe
Lime	All essences in concentrated form

MILK AND ORANGE

½ pint Milk
2 teaspoonfuls Sugar
1 Orange
  Squeeze out the juice of the Orange, and strain it into a tumbler. Add the Sugar and the cold Milk.

FRUIT MILK DRINKS

MILK POSSET

½ pint Milk
1 tablespoonful of Golden Syrup or Honey
Bring the Milk to the boil, and stir in the Syrup
or Honey.

MILK TEA

½ pint Milk
2 teaspoonfuls Tea
Put the Tea into a jug, boil Milk and pour on.
Stand for three to five minutes keeping hot. Strain
into a cup.

INVALID DRINKS

INVALID DRINKS

AMERICAN CRUST COFFEE

Cut some thin slices of stale bread, and bake them in the oven until they are quite dark brown. Pound them in a mortar. Boil one ounce of the crumbs in half a pint of water in a small saucepan. Take it off the fire, let it stand for a few minutes, and then strain the liquid through a fine strainer into a breakfast cup. Serve hot.

APPLE WATER

Cut three large Apples, unpared, in slices, pour a quart of boiling water over them, cover, and leave until quite cold. Strain, add a very little Sugar and a squeeze of Lemon.

Or

Boil the sliced Apples with the water and a strip of Lemon peel for an hour. Then cover the jug until the liquid is quite cold. Strain, and add a very little powdered Sugar.

INVALID DRINKS

BARLEY WATER

Wash and blanch two ounces of Pearl Barley, add the grated rind and the juice of a Lemon and an ounce of Sugar. Pour over a quart of boiling water, cover, and leave until cold. Strain and use.

BARLEY WATER (THICK)

Wash and blanch two ounces Pearl Barley, strain, rinse it and put it with the thinly cut rind of half a Lemon and a quart of cold water into a double saucepan, where it must boil gently for an hour to two hours. Then add the juice of half a Lemon and Sugar to taste. Strain and use when cold.

Note. The barley is blanched by being put into cold water, brought to the boil and boiled for one minute.

BLACK CURRANT TEA

Boil two tablespoonfuls of Black Currant jam with a quart of water for half an hour. Thicken it then, if you like, with a quarter of a teaspoonful of cornflour mixed with a little water and boiled with the Tea for three minutes. Strain and use.

Or

More simply still, just pour half a pint of boiling water over a tablespoonful of Black Currant jam.

INVALID DRINKS

CAUDLE (I)

Beat an Egg to a froth, and add it to a mixture of a pint of Gruel, a glass of Sherry, and Lemon rind and Sugar to taste.

CAUDLE (II)

Make half a pint of rather thick Gruel, and while it is boiling add a glass of Port Wine and Lemon to taste. Let it get cool, and beat into it a stiffly whisked Egg white.

A COUGH MIXTURE

Mix together:
1 gill Whisky
4 oz. Honey
2 oz. Glycerine
The juice of two Lemons

EGG AND SODA WATER

Beat together a new laid Egg yolk and a teaspoonful of Castor Sugar until thick and creamy. Mix well with this two tablespoonfuls of Milk. Pour into a glass and add a gill of Soda Water.

The white can also be used, if desired, but it must be stiffly whisked before it is added.

INVALID DRINKS

EGG FLIP

Beat an Egg well in a bowl. Warm a glass of
Milk in a saucepan, without bringing it to the boil,
dissolve in it Sugar to your taste, add a teaspoonful
of Brandy, and pour it on to the Egg, whipping
well.

FEVER DRINK

Roast six good baking Apples. When they are
done, put them into a jug, pour over them three
pints of boiling water, cover the jug closely, and
when it is cold it is ready to drink. Add a spoonful
of Honey or Sugar.

GRUEL

Mix an ounce of medium ground Oatmeal with
half a pint of water, cover it and let it stand for an
hour. Then stir it up and strain it into a saucepan,
stir it over the fire until boiling, and then simmer
it for a quarter of an hour. Salt or sweeten to taste
before serving.

LEMON POSSET (MRS. ROUNDELL)

Put a good handful of breadcrumbs into a
quart of water, simmer it to a pint, with a strip

of Lemon peel boiled in it. Add the juice of a Lemon, four Eggs, and a gill of Sherry. Stir well, and add the Eggs off the fire. Warm the posset up, and sweeten it a little. For a cold.

PORT WINE DRINK

Two glasses of Port and two Eggs well beaten up in half a pint of Milk. Sweeten if liked. Strain before serving.

Burgundy can be treated (ill treated?) in the same way.

PRAIRIE OYSTER

Put a teaspoonful of Wine Vinegar in a wine-glass, break a new laid Egg into it, add a little Pepper and Salt, and swallow at a gulp.

QUEEN CHARLOTTE'S CAUDLE

Stir a pint of cold water into half a pint of Oatmeal, and strain through a fine strainer into a saucepan. Add a gill of Gin, and the same quantity of Mild Ale, a few Raisins, a grated Nutmeg, a little ground Ginger, and a little Sugar. Boil for ten minutes, and serve hot to the company in cups.

INVALID DRINKS

RAISIN JUICE

Simmer a pound and a half seedless Raisins in four pints of water, until the Raisins change colour. Then squeeze and strain, and bottle.

SAGE TEA

Put half an ounce of dried Sage leaves in a jar, fill with a quart of boiling water, and add Sugar and Lemon juice to taste.

STOORUM

A drink for nursing mothers. Put a heaped teaspoonful of Oatmeal into a tumbler; pour a little cold water over it and stir well. Fill up half-way with boiling water, then to the top with boiling Milk. Season with Salt and serve.

TEA MADE WITH MILK

Make Tea in the usual way with a teaspoonful of Tea and half a pint of Milk. But let it stand one minute only, when it must be poured out and served at once.

TOAST WATER

Toast the crust of a loaf of bread on each side.

Pour over it a quart of cold water. When the colour of Sherry, strain and serve.

TOAST AND WATER

'Toasted Oatcake', it is said, 'with boiling water poured over makes quite the best flavoured toast and water.'

TREACLE POSSET

Boil half a pint of Milk, add two tablespoonfuls of Treacle or Golden Syrup, bring to the boil again, strain and use.

WHITE WINE WHEY

Bring half a pint of Milk to the boil, add a glass of Sherry, stir together, add a teaspoonful of Castor Sugar, let it dissolve, and then strain. It should be drunk very hot.

APPENDIX

A SHORT BIBLIOGRAPHY OF BOOKS DEALING
WITH DRINK WHICH ARE IN PRINT
(see page 155)

'ADRIAN'
Cocktail Fashions of 1936   Simpkin, Marshall

ALLEN, H. WARNER
Gentlemen, I give you—Wine   Faber
Rum (Criterion Miscellany)   Faber
Sherry   Constable
Wines of France, The   Benn

ANON
688 Recipes for Drinks   Jenkins

AYE, F.
Wines and Wisdom   Universal Publications

BERRY, CHARLES WALTER
In Search of Wine   Constable
Viniana   Constable

BOULESTIN, X. MARCEL
What shall we have to Drink?   Heinemann

APPENDIX

BUNYARD, EDWARD A.
  Anatomy of Dessert, The   Chatto
  Epicure's Companion, The   Dent

DE CASSAGNAC, P.
  French Wines   Chatto

CRADDOCK, H.
  Savoy Cocktail Book, The   Constable

CRAIG, ELIZABETH
  Wine in the Kitchen   Constable

DE FLEURY, R.
  1800 and All That   St. Catherine's Press

'DRINKER, A'
  A Book about Beer   Cape

FOOTE, E. J.
  Will you take Wine?   Pitman

FORBES, ELLERT
  Wines for Everyman   Herbert Joseph

'GOURMET'
  Gourmet's Book of Food and Drink John Lane

GWYNN, STEPHEN
  Burgundy   Constable

HEALY, MAURICE
  Claret and the White Wines of Bordeaux
                       Constable

HEATH, AMBROSE
  Dining Out   Eyre & Spottiswoode

APPENDIX

JACK, FLORENCE B.
  100 Drinks and Cups   Country Life
  100 Home-brewed Wines   Country Life

LLOYD, F. C.
  Art and Technique of Wine, The   Constable

MEIER, F.
  Artistry of Mixing Drinks, The
                      Fryam Press, Paris

'ROBERT'
  Cocktails and How to Make Them   Jenkins

RUDD, H. R.
  Hocks and Moselles   Constable

SAINTSBURY, G.
  Notes on a Cellar Book   Macmillan

SCHOONMAKER AND MARVEL
  Complete Wine Book, The   Routledge

SHAND, P. MORTON
  Book of other Wines than French, A. Knopf

SIMON, ANDRÉ L.
  Blood of the Grape, The   Duckworth
  Champagne   Constable
  Dictionary of Wine, A   Cassell
  Port   Constable
  Tables of Content   Constable

SIMON, ANDRÉ L. AND CRAIG, ELIZA-
    BETH
  Madeira, Cakes and Sauce   Constable

APPENDIX

STEEDMAN and SENN
Home-made Summer and Winter Drinks
Ward, Lock

TARLING, W. J.
Café Royal Cocktail Book, The
43 Duke Street, S.W.1

TODD, W. J.
Handbook of Wine, A   Cape
Port, How to Buy, Serve, and Drink   Cape

WELBY, T. EARLE
Cellar Key, The   Gollancz

WINE AND FOOD SOCIETY, THE
Wine and Food *passim*
(The Society's Quarterly Journal)
Wine and Food Society
Wines and Liqueurs, A to Z
Wine and Food Society

WOODMAN, MARY
Cocktails and American Drinks, etc.   Foulsham

THE AUTHORS OF THE
QUOTATIONS ON PAGES 13-16

1. Sheridan.
2. Masefield.
3. H. S. Leigh (*Stanzas to an Intoxicated Fly*).
4. Robert Hall, D.D. (*Life*).
5. Shakespeare (*Henry IV*, Part 2).
6. Henry Aldridge, D.D.
7. Latin Epigram from which the above is translated.
8. Shakespeare (*Henry IV*, Part 2).
9. Congreve.
10. Oliver Wendell Holmes.
11. Thomas Love Peacock.
12. Disraeli (*Sybil*).
13. Dickens (*Pickwick Papers*).
14. Thomas Hood.
15. Hilaire Belloc.
16. C. S. Calverley.
17. Epitaph at Winchester.
18. From 'Oxford Nightcaps', quoted in *Hone's Year Book*.
19. Dickens (*David Copperfield*).
20. Boswell's *Johnson*.
21. Thackeray.
22. *Life of Morland, the Painter.*
23. Thomas Moore.
24. G. K. Chesterton.
25. Hilaire Belloc (*The Four Men*).

CLASSIFIED INDEX

HARD DRINKS

COCKTAILS

Absinthe, 21
Alexandra, 21
American Beauty, 21
Angel Face, 22
Applejack (1), 22
Applejack (2), 22
Apricot, 22
Baron, 22
Belmont, 23
Bentley, 23
Bitter Sweet, 23
Bloodhound, 23
Blue Devil, 24
Bobby Burns, 24
Bombay, 24
Bosom Caresser, 24
Brandy, 25
Brandy Cocktail, 25
Brandy Vermouth, 25
Brave New World, 25
Bronx, 26
Bronx, Silver, 26

Calvados, 26
Champagne, 26
Cinzano, 26
Clover Club, 27
Corpse Reviver, 27
Creole, 27
Daiquiri, 27
Devil's Kiss, 27
Dubonnet, 28
Gin, 28
Gin and Cape, 28
Gin-and-It, 28
Gin and Mixed, 28
Golf, 29
Grapefruit, 29
Green Room, 29
Hollywood, 29
Homestead, 29
Honey Orange, 30
Hong Kong Special, 30
Knockout, 30
Maiden's Blush, 30
Maiden's Prayer, 30

231

CLASSIFIED INDEX

COCKTAILS

Manhattan (Sweet), 31
Manhattan (Dry), 31
Marmalade, 31
Martini (Dry) (1), 31
Martini (Dry) (2), 32
Martini (Sweet), 32
Martini (Medium), 32
Monkey Gland, 32
Orange Blossom, 32
Paradise, 32
Pegu Club, 33
Perfect, 33
Philadelphia, 33
Piccadilly, 33
Pink Gin, 33
Pink Lady, 34
Planters (1), 34
Planters (2), 34
Port Wine, 34
Public Enemy No. 1, 34
Quaglino's Special, 35
Quelle Vie, 35
Rainbow, 35
Rob Roy, 36
Rose (1), 36
Rose (2), 36
Royal Romance, 36
Satan's Whiskers (Straight), 36
Satan's Whiskers (Curled), 37
Saucy Sue, 37
Scarlet Lady, 37

Self-Starter, 37
Sherry, 38
Sherry and Bitters, 38
Sidecar, 38
Sloe Gin, 38
Thunder and Lightning, 38
Tomato, 39
Trinity, 39
Turf Club, 39
Vermouth, 39
Waldorf, 40
Whisky, 40
White Lady, 40
Will Rogers, 40

COLD DRINKS (HARD)

Allahabad Tankard, 43
American Egg-Nogg, 43
American Glory, 43
American Lemonade, 44
Apricot Cooler, 44
Asses' Milk, 44
A Summer Beverage, 44
Auld Man's Milk, 45
Automobile Cooler, 45
Badminton, 45
Barbadoes Swizzle, 45
Black Velvet, 46
Bosom Caresser, 46
Boston Cooler, 46
Brandy Shake, 46
Brandy Smash, 47
Bull Dog, 47

HARD DRINKS

Bull's Milk, 47
Champagne Cobbler, 47
Ching-Ching, 48
Cider Egg-Nogg, 48
Cider Posset, 48
Claret Lemonade, 48
Cloudy Sky, 49
Coca-Cola Highball, 49
Collins, Tom, 49
Collins, John, 50
Collins, Rye, 50
Collins, Scotch, 50
Collins, Irish, 50
Collins, Rum, 50
Collins, Brandy, 50
Country Club Cooler, 50
Eau de Fraises, 50
Egg and Brandy Drink, 51
Eton Blazer, 51
Floster, 52
Gimlet, 52
Gin and Beer, 52
Gin and Coca-Cola, 52
Gin and Ginger Ale or Beer, 53
Gin Rickey, 53
Gin-Sling, (2) 53
Gin-Sling (2), 54
Havelock, 54
Horse's Neck (Stiff), 54
Iced Coffee Variant, 54
Imperial, 54
John Bright, 55

Kardinal, 55
King's Peg, 55
Knickerbocker, 55
Lemonade (1), 56
Lemonade (2), 56
Lemonade (3), 56
Lone Tree Cooler, 57
Mahogany, 57
Maitrank, 57
Mint Cooler, 57
Mint Drink, 58
Mint Julep, 58
Mother-in-law, 58
Mother's Milk, 58
Night-Cap, 59
Peach and Honey, 59
Pineapple Julep, 59
Planter's Breakfast, 59
Polichinelle, 60
Port and Lemon, 60
Rajah's Peg, 60
Raspberry Nectar, 60
Rum Shake, 60
Russian Velvet, 61
Saint Charles, 61
Shady Grove Cooler, 61
Shandy Gaff, 61
Sherry and Lemon, 62
Sherry Blush, 62
Sherry Cobbler, 62
Sherry Drink, 62
Sherry Sangaree, 62
Sifter, 63

CLASSIFIED INDEX

COLD DRINKS (HARD)

Sleepy Head, 63
Sloe Gin Rickey, 63
Spider, 63
Spike Lemonade, 63
Stone Fence, 64
Straight Scotch Highball, 64
Summer Drink, 64
Surgeon-Major, 64
Tewahdiddle, 65
Twist, 65
Uncle, 65
Velvet Blush, 65

HOT DRINKS (HARD)

Ale Posset, 69
Bishop (1), 69
Bishop (2), 70
Blue Blazer, 71
Brown Caudle, 71
Burnt Coffee, 71
Churchwarden, 72
Egg Flip, 72
Glögg, 72
Glühwein, 73
Het Pint, 73
Home Ruler, 73
Honeysuckle, 73
Hot Spiced Ale, 74
Lamb's Wool, 74
Lawn Sleeves, 74
Le Brulo, 75
Locomotive, 75

Mulled Ale, 75
Mulled Wine, 76
Negus (1), 76
Negus (2), 76
Negus White Wine, 77
Night-Cap, 77
Purl, 77
Scots Aleberry, 71
Sleeper, 77
Uncle Toby, 78
Vin Chaud, 78
Wassail Bowl, 78
Whisky Toddy, 79

CUPS (HARD)

Ale, 83
Ale (John's Nectar), 83
A Mixed Cup, 83
Apricot, 84
Bacchus, 84
Beer, 84
Bull's Eye, 85
Burgundy, 85
Champagne, 85
Champagne (Simple), 86
Cider (1), 86
Cider (2), 86
Cider (3), 86
Claret (1), 87
Claret (2), 87
Claret (3), 88
Claret (Nathaniel Gubbins), 88

234

HARD DRINKS

Claret (Austrian), 88
Claret (Prof. Saintsbury's), 89
Club, 89
Eskrick Park, 89
Hock (1), 90
Hock (2), 90
Hock (3), 91
Institution, 91
King, 91
Liqueur, 92
Loving, 92
Merton College Cider, 93
Mint, 93
Moselle, 93
Peach, 93
Peach (Adalor), 94
Port Wine, 94
Red Currant, 94
Sherry (1), 94
Sherry (2), 95
Sherry (Prof. Saintsbury's), 95
Strawberry, 95
Turk's Neck, 96

PUNCHES (HARD)

Barbadoes, 99
Cherry, 99
Cider, 99
Devil's Cup, 100
Fish House, 100
Gin, 101
Glasgow, 101

Lager Beer, 101
Marquise, 102
Milk, 102
Mint, 102
Norfolk, 103
Old English, 103
Peach, 103
Pfirsichbowle, 104
Punch with Kirsch, 104
Rum Punch, 105
Rum Punch (Prof. Saintsbury), 105
Summer, 105
Swedish Punsch, 106

LIQUEURS, a short list of, 111-12

HOME-MADE DRINKS

Athole Brose, 115
Birch Wine, 115
Blackberry Brandy, 116
Blackberry Cordial, 116
Blackberry Vinegar, 116
Black Currant Cordial, 117
Bramble Tip Wine, 117
Cherry Bounce, 118
Cherry Brandy, 118
Cherry Cordial, 118
Cherry Wine, 118
Cider, 119
Clove Brandy, 119
Crab Apple Wine, 119

CLASSIFIED INDEX

HOME-MADE DRINKS

Damson Gin, 120
Dandelion Wine, 120
Cowslip Wine, 121
Cranberry Cordial, 121
Elderflower Champagne, 122
Ginger Beer (1), 122
Ginger Beer (2), 123
Ginger Cordial, 123
Gooseberry Wine, 124
Grape Cordial, 124
Grape Wine, 124
Green Gooseberry Wine, 126
Hawthorn Berry Wine, 126
Highland Cordial, 126
Lemon Brandy, 127
Lemon Gin, 127
Mangel-Wurzel Wine, 127
Mulberry Brandy, 128
Nectar, 128
Nettle Beer, 129
Orange Brandy, 129
Orange Gin, 130
Orange Wine, 130
Plum Wine, 130
Quince Wine, 131
Raspberry Vinegar, 131
Ratafia of Apricots, 132
Ratafia of Peaches, 132
Rhubarb Champagne, 132
Sherry Tonic, 133
Shrub, 133

Sloe Gin, 133
Strawberry Liqueur, 134
Tomato Wine, 134
Whortleberry Wine, 135

VEGETABLE WINES

Beetroot, 139
Carrot, 139
Parsley, 140
Parsnip, 140
Pea-Pod, 141
Potato, 142
Rhubarb, 143
Rhubarb Brandy, 142
Swede, 143
Tomato, 144
Turnip, 144

CURIOUS DRINKS

Brazil Relish, 147
Bunnyhug Cocktail, 147
Cocktail (Francatelli), 147
Cure for Drunkenness, 147
Drink for the Fidgets, 148
Farmer's Joy, 148
Hock Cup, 148
King William's Posset, 149
Kitty Highball, 149
Mountain Oyster, 149
Pick-me-Up, 149
Prima Donna, 150
Scorcher, 150
Split Worcester, 150

SOFT DRINKS

Texas Highball, 150
Thunderclap Cocktail, 150
Tiger's Milk (1), 151
Tiger's Milk (2), 151

Wait a Bit, 151

WINE, A Note on, 155

SOFT DRINKS

COCKTAILS

Choirboy, 161
Clam Juice, 161
Fruit Juice, 161
Ginger, 162
Lemon, 162
Lime Juice, 162
Orange, 163
Parson's Special, 163
Prairie Hen, 163
Sauerkraut Juice, 163
Three Fruit, 163
Tomato (1), 164
Tomato (2), 164
Tomato (3), 165

COLD DRINKS (SOFT)

A Fruit Drink (1), 169
A Fruit Drink (2), 169
Almond Water, 170
A Long Fruit Drink, 170
Apple Tree Dulcet, 170
Blackberry Drink, 171
Canton Lemonade, 171
Cherry Drink (1), 171
Cherry Drink (2), 171

Eau de Fraises, 50
Figs and Apples, 172
Ginger Ale and Angostura, 172
Grape Juice, 172
Grape Juice and Ginger Ale, 173
Grenadine Frappé, 173
Horse's Neck (Dispirited), 173
Iced Chocolate, 173
Iced Tea, 174
Jam Fruit Drinks, various, 174
Lemonade, 175
Lemonade (American), 175
Mint Cooler, 175
Mulberry Drink, 175
Mule's Collar, 176
Orangeade (1), 176
Orangeade (2), 176
Orange and Honey, 177
Persian Sherbet, 177
Pineapple Fizz, 177
Prune Water, 178
Rhubarb Flip, 178

CLASSIFIED INDEX

COLD DRINKS (SOFT)

Sarsaparilla Cooler, 178
Sarsaparilla Drink, 179
Strawberry Drink, 179

HOT DRINKS (SOFT)

Chocolate (Swedish), 183
Cocoa-Nibs, 183
Lait de Poule, 184
Lemonade, Hot Spiced, 184
Mexican Chocolate, 184
Raisin Tea, 185

CUPS (SOFT)

Apple, 189
Fruit, 189
Ginger Ale, 190
Grapefruit and Orange, 190
Pussyfoot, 190

PUNCHES (SOFT)

Cardinal, 195
Chocolate, 195
Elderberry, 195
German (American Style), 196
Iced Tea Punch, 196
Orange, 196
Mint Fruit, 197
Mulberry, 197
Pomegranate, 198

Red Currant, 197
Tea, 198

COLD MILK DRINKS

Milk Shake, 203
Apple Blossom, 203
Banana Cream Whip, 203
Chocolate Milk Shake (1), 204
Chocolate Milk Shake (2), 204
Coffee Milk Shake, 204
Cream Snowball, 205
Fruit Salad Shake, 205
Ginger Frappé, 205
Loganberry Delight, 206
Pineapple Milk Frappé, 206

HOT MILK DRINKS

Apricot Fluff, 209
Autumn Glory, 209
Caramel Cream Whip, 209
Egg Maraschino, 210
Egyptian Flip, 210
Milk Ambrosia, 210
Savoury Shake, 211

FRUIT MILK DRINKS

Fruit Milk Drink, 215
Milk and Orange, 215
Milk Posset, 215
Milk Tea, 216

SOFT DRINKS

INVALID DRINKS

American Crust Coffee, 219
Apple Water, 219
Barley Water, 220
Barley Water (Thick), 220
Black Currant Tea, 220
Caudle (1), 221
Caudle (2), 221
Cough Mixture, 221
Egg and Soda Water, 221
Egg Flip, 222
Fever Drink, 222
Gruel, 222

Lemon Posset, 222
Port Wine Drink, 223
Prairie Oyster, 223
Queen Charlotte's Caudle, 223
Raisin Juice, 224
Sage Tea, 224
Stoorum, 224
Tea made with Milk, 224
Toast Water, 224-5
Treacle Posset, 225
White Wine Whey, 225